PINK ZINNIA

Pink Zinnia

Poems and Stories

Franklin Abbott

authorHOUSE®

AuthorHouse™
1663 Liberty Drive, Suite 200
Bloomington, IN 47403
www.authorhouse.com
Phone: 1-800-839-8640

First published by AuthorHouse 7/1/2009

ISBN: 978-1-4389-5695-4 (sc)

Library of Congress Control Number: 2009901792

Printed in the United States of America
Bloomington, Indiana

This book is printed on acid-free paper.

Cover Photos Copyright (c) 2009 by Seth Grad

Some of these poems appeared in Van Gogh's Ear and RFD and on the web on sites for Atlanta Rainbow Muse, White Crane and the Georgia Society for Clinical Social Work's Clinical Page and Outside the Green Zone: Poets respond to the GLBT Cleansing of Iraq.

www.pinkzinniapoems.com

in memory of my grandparents

Homer Claude and Jewell Chandler Abbott

John Wallis and Christine Watson Carpenter

Que devient le rêvê quand le rêvê est fini?
(What becomes of the dream when the dream is over?)

inscription on the grave of Serge Peretti
1905 - 1997
Premier Danseur Étoile
de L'Opera de Paris
Pére Lachaise Cemetery

PREFACE

The decision to self-publish my book was an easy one. It is more prestigious when a major publisher or even a small, respected one, publishes your book but the hassles are rarely worth the reward especially for a book of poetry. In the United States, poetry has become more and more the province of academics. They dominate the journals and small presses and, understandably, bank their careers on publication; just like every other faculty member, they must publish or perish.

Jane Yolen in her wonderful book for writers, *Take Joy*, showed me a different way of looking at publication. She said that to publish is simply to proclaim in public. Taking that to heart, I have made good use of the Internet and email to disseminate my poems. When I was younger and a letter writer, I would often include copies of my poems in missives to friends. My letters and those of my friends who were writers always weighed more. In addition to poems I could enclose feathers or shells, a dried flower or leaf, a pretty piece of fabric, photographs and newspaper clippings. Every now and then I receive or send such a letter and it is always a pleasure to do so. Of course email lends itself to attachments and distribution lists make it easy to send something far and wide with the click of a key, but I miss the feel of paper, the design of stationery, the look of stamps and post marks, and the occasional little surprises that would fall from letters as they were opened.

For me it is gratifying to share my creativity with friends and to receive in return their comments and - even better - their own creative renderings. This has been a great source of inspiration, and I am grateful to all my friends for the warmth of their encouragement. It is important for me (as it is for most creative people) to engage an audience, even a virtual one. It is also important to me to have artifacts, hence this book. I want to hold it in my hands and put it in your hands. I want it to exist as an object on our bookshelves and in libraries and so I am taking this next step.

I have many people to thank but must limit myself to mentioning a few; my memory being my memory I will surely omit someone important, so let me say simply that I am grateful to feel such kinship with so many. A big part of my push to write and publish has come from my writing group, The Ninth Muse. We meet monthly and comfort and cajole each other to keep fingers moving across keyboards, pens moving across paper, and images emerging from our waking dreams. My fellow muses, LaDonna Benedict, Jill Knueppel, Barbara Locascio, Emily Simerly and Pat "Wren" Wells, along with former muses Kelly Stone and Craig Storlie, have been and continue to be such good company on the creative journey. I am also very lucky to be a part of the creative life of my city and my queer community. The voices of younger poets and writers revitalize me and the gifts of my peers and elders keep me humble and grateful. My work coordinating community readings at Outwrite Bookstore and the Atlanta Queer Literary Festival at the Atlanta/Fulton Public libraries (special thanks to Philip Rafshoon, Richard Cruce, Cal Gough, Collin Kelley, and Megan Volpert) has kept me in continuous contact with a vibrant and diverse group of writers whom I never tire of hearing. I am also lucky to have friends who have taken time to show me the wonders of their worlds: Martha Ham in Utah, Stéphane Korsia in Paris, Ashok Kumar and Acha Kamath in India. My love of travel has always been charmed by the people I encounter, some of whom you will meet in these pages.

One more set of thank you's: to Ioana Rican who helped me prepare the manuscript, Gabi Rican for his technical support and encouragement, Seth Grad for the cover photos, and Roger Bailey and Cal Gough for editorial assistance. Special thanks to Guerin Asante for his encouragement and love. A final thank you to you who are reading these words right now. We may or may not have met or will meet in person. I hope that what I share will in some way move you to share your own stories and poems. This is a big part of what makes us human and what makes the human experience worthwhile. The novelist Isak Dinesen wrote, "all sorrows can be borne if you put them into a story." I believe her. I also believe that joy is infectious and the more we share it the more we know it.

Franklin Abbott
9 November 2008
Stone Mountain, Georgia

Contents

BURIAL IN BIRMINGHAM

Burial in Birmingham

I am not part of history. I am part of mystery.
                                        -- Sun Ra
I am bigger than my body.
                                        -- John Mayer

My paternal grandmother, Jesse Jewell Chandler Abbott, was buried a week ago today in Elmwood Cemetery in Birmingham, Alabama. She died early in the morning the Wednesday before in the hospital in Punta Gorda, Florida. She was 101 on her last birthday, February 10th.

My parents had called the night before the funeral to warn me to leave early. It was the big race weekend in Talladega and the super speedway was right off the interstate between Atlanta and Birmingham. I did get up early and checked my email with my morning coffee, as usual. As serendipity would have it, the word of the day which comes every day from Merriam-Webster was "bereft." It is a word derived from the Old English *bereafian* meant to rob or plunder. *Bereafian* became bereaved, to have something taken from you, to be bereft. I felt the word.

Just as I left my home it began to rain and rain hard and did so unabated until I got to Alabama. I stopped at the State Line Fuel Center to fill the tank and empty my bladder. On the way to the restroom I noticed a boiled peanut dispenser (Regular and Cajun) and a case of hot biscuits enclosing various meats including bologna. I asked the woman at the cash register if it was raining in Birmingham and she replied that she didn't know anything about anywhere other than here. Her deadpan insularity reassured me that I was in fact in Alabama.

The rain was dissipating, turning into mist as I crossed the Coosa River. The phalanx of traffic my parents had warned against failed to materialize. When I got to Talladega I understood why. Encamped around the super speedway was a veritable army of RV's. The throngs had already arrived for what looked to be a redneck Woodstock. The super speedway covers 2000 acres and looks like an attenuated football stadium from afar. Over 150,000 fans watched as racing cars flew around the 2.66 mile tri-oval race track. Miss America sang the national anthem. Jeff Gordon, who began his racing career at age 5, won the race for the fourth time.

Past the speedway, I entered the Talladega National Forest and the misting rain became a cloud. I could see the trees in ghostly silhouette, the white daisies and pink poppies on the roadside. I went past Eden and Odenville, Pell City, Cook Springs and Chula Vista. I crossed the Cahaba River and drove past small towns named Moody, Leeds, and Irondale, places where people were too old or too poor to move on. As I drove into Birmingham the clouds held their moisture and I went south on Interstate 65 and exited on 6th Street. The bail bond shops that lined the road indicated I was close to the Birmingham jail where my grandfather, Homer Abbott, now dead thirteen years, had worked as a police officer and detective in the 30's and 40's, and where Martin Luther King, Jr. had been incarcerated and wrote his famous *Letter from the Birmingham Jail*. 6th Street dead ends into Martin Luther King, Jr. Drive, the western boundary of Elmwood Cemetery.

Elmwood is the largest and best-known cemetery in Birmingham. Lots of politicians are buried there, as are jazz iconoclast Sun Ra and Eddie Kendricks of the Temptations. The most famous person buried at Elmwood is Paul "Bear" Bryant who had been head coach of football at the University of Alabama. During the glory days of his team, the Crimson Tide, Bryant had been the virtual Emperor of Alabama. Three quarters of a million people lined the funeral route from Tuscaloosa to Birmingham to pay their respects as his cortege passed. His grave, though modest, is a pilgrimage site for admirers who leave behind bottles of Coca Cola and packages of Golden Flake potato chips (he endorsed these products) in his memory. All of my grandparents are now buried at Elmwood, my grandmother was buried next to her husband Homer, and head to head with her mother who was known as

4

Mother Gable, who died three days short of my third birthday in the early fifties.

The funeral home was the same one used for my other grandparents' funerals. My grandmother is in Parlor C which is where my mother's mother had been fifteen years before. Since I left early I am the first to arrive and am escorted by one of the staff to Parlor C. I called my grandmother Nana and there she is in a silver casket. She has always seemed ancient to me and seems the same only asleep on white pillows in the silver box. She was a gardener and loved to go fishing and her skin has always been deeply wrinkled. Her white hair was always curled and permed and had been for this occasion. It was odd to be here alone but I was grateful to have the time to say the things I knew she knew. I thanked her for her long, loving presence in my life. Our relationship had been simple, strong and close, something we lived but rarely talked about. Her love came through in her cooking and hospitality which were legendary. She was born and raised in the country north of Birmingham and had little formal education. She married Homer when she was young and they soon moved to Birmingham to have a life other than farming. Homer trained to be a barber but was very bad at it and became a policeman instead. My grandmother stayed home cared for my grandfather and assorted relatives and raised two children though the Depression and war years.

Parlor C is a small green room. The furniture is French pretentious. There are chairs, a sofa, two end tables; one with a small white ceramic bust of Napoleon, the other with a matching bust of Josephine. It is at the end of the corridor and the door is open. I see my parents walking down the hall toward me. They look older than they ever have. My aunt is with them and soon after friends and neighbors begin arriving. A couple of distant cousins follow and then my brother, his wife and their two grown sons. We are waiting for the minister who is late. Finally a funeral director locates him at the grave site and brings him up to Parlor C.

Brother Preacher is from the Beechwood Baptist Church in Mt. Olive, Alabama where my grandmother had lived until she was moved to Florida and assisted living. He had known my grandmother, she was a church member, and had visited her in her home on Meadowview Lane. He prayed with us and then launched into his theme: my grandmother was in A Better Place. He read about Heaven from the Book of Revelations, the controversial book tacked on to the end of the New Testament three hundred years after the death of Jesus. It was written by a paranoid hermit who lived in a cave on a Greek island who never met the long-dead Jesus or any of his disciples. It is a rambling hallucination mostly scary and very useful when religion is used to control people. Brother Preacher did not tell us that the description of heaven he read to us (Revelations 21:10-27) was offered by one of the seven angels who had the seven bowls full of the seven last plagues. But the description of heaven was grand: pearly gates, streets of gold, walls lined with jasper, sapphires, onyx, topaz, and amethysts. Somewhere in the midst of this a scruffy young couple came to the door and stood looking nervous and out of place. My grandmother's only great granddaughter Britta had arrived with her fiancé.

I was one of six pall bearers. We maneuvered the casket into the hearse and followed it down through the cemetery to a hill where a tent had been erected. The funeral director, a slight young man with a buzz hair cut told us it was okay to step on other people's graves as we carried Nana's casket up to the tent and positioned it on a gurney. It was windy and all but a few of us went back to the funeral home. I stayed and placed a bouquet of pink statice, the pinkest flower I could find (pink being Nana's favorite color) on the coffin and watched as it was lowered into the earth.

There were three men in the burial detail. The first I saw was an older black man with three bags under each eye and the aura of hard living or hard luck, the next was a younger black man who had two bags under each eye and a similar vibration. Their supervisor was also African American but looked less oppressed. What distinguished him was that he was a dwarf. The funeral director came over to make small talk and asked me what I did for a living. It is often a mistake to tell people you are a psychotherapist and I made that mistake. There are usually two responses. One is to inquire about all the "really crazy" people I work with hoping in doing so to fish out some entertainment. I don't tell them that suffering is as ubiquitous as the dirt we walk on and demur behind the veil of confidentiality. The other tact is taken by the funeral director, who begins telling me his secrets like I am a coin collector and he is showing me a rare dime. I learn that he is on Lexipro and that he is transitioning from being an airplane mechanic to being a nurse and he is doing funeral directing as a segue. I learn he has a pregnant wife and a two year old child so it doesn't matter that the Lexipro is producing sexual side effects because it helps him cope with his wife who gets so "hormonal" that she flies into rages and throws him out when he has done "nothing at all." This is all spoken in a high-pitched half-whisper that sounds like a mosquito buzzing in my ear. I am about at saturation when I am rescued by my cousin Britta, her fiancé, and my nephew John.

Britta is twenty-one, petite and pretty. She looks like a little bird. Her fiancé apologizes for their attire, both explain that they thought there would be only a few people at the funeral, that they had been in a hurry. Britta is holding a piece of paper and says she had written a poem that she did not read at the service. I ask her to read it now. She calls my grandmother, her great-grandmother, her "abbott" and metamorphs her into "a pink flower." She says she always felt her love and acceptance no matter what. I know exactly what she means. She has to go or be late for work. She works with livestock in a pet store and is an expert on setting up aquariums and vivavariums. She draws the line with poison tree frogs, saying it's not the kind of work she wants to die for.

My nephew John, a tall gentle young man in his early twenties, and I are left at the graveside watching the tent being taken down and the gurney disassembled. I want to wait until the green fake Astroturf is removed from the gravesides to see the red Alabama earth that will hold Nana's body. John is as pagan-hearted as I am and has brought sunflower seeds to toss in the grave. My grandmother had been very proud of the sunflowers she grew that were over twice her height. Nana had been a natural pagan. She was a nominal Christian but never talked about religion or read the Bible. She would always insist that we begin meals without a prayer saying she blessed the food when she cooked it. She did go to church but her chief delight there was decorating the altar with flowers from her garden. She told me that once in a bad drought she hung a rattlesnake she killed in a tree to bring rain. I asked her if it worked. She nodded, "sure did," then laughed, having amused herself.

I joined the rest of the family back at the funeral home and went to lunch with my brother, his wife, my parents and, my aunt. We talked about the ordinary, ordinary stuff of life. Only once was my grandmother mentioned. My Aunt Sue had been with her in the hospital shortly before she died and said that my grandmother told her she had seen my grandfather standing by her bedside. This was a relief to my aunt who reminded us that Nana's stubborn refusal to leave Meadowview Lane was due to her concerns that Homer wouldn't know where to find her when it was time for her to join him. I couldn't get down to Florida before my grandmother's death but was advised by a friend who works with hospice that I could communicate with her from afar by sending thoughts and images through visualization. Nana and Homer had spent many happy years in a little white house on the Bon Secour River in south Alabama. They had a pier for their boat and I sent her an image of being on the pier and seeing a boat coming from across the river. My grandfather and her brothers Duke and E.C. were in the boat and they were coming to get her.

After lunch I dropped my aunt at the airport and drove back to Atlanta through more rain. When I got home I stretched and showered and sat in the quiet of the evening thinking and not thinking, being with my bereavement. In the still of the night I hear a bird singing outside my window, *sheeshere, sheeshere*. The mockingbird sounds a grace note at the end of this long Saturday and I feel my grandmother as a presence in and around me.

A friend wrote in a condolence note that it was hard when you lose someone who has been a fixed point in your life your whole life long. While I appreciate that my grandmother became transparent in degrees as she lived beyond old into ancient I am struck with how true it is that her loss leaves me without a guiding star. I feel more vulnerable to the gravity that will someday engulf me. For several nights my dreams are topsy turvy and my sleep fitful. A week after the night she died I dream of her. She is not transparent at all but saturated with color. She is living in a cottage deep in the woods and when I tell her of my problems with sleep she pulls a wooden wheel tray from under her bed that has colored pebbles in its hollows. She selects two small blue and green ones and tells me she is going to scotch tape them under my shoulder blades. I wake from the dream briefly and then fall into a deep sleep that lasts for hours.

I imagine my grandmother in her own kind of heaven. She is gardening and fishing and cooking up a storm for all the hungry relatives and neighbors who have been waiting for her arrival. If her heaven is the same one that Brother Preacher described then it is a better place for her being there. God is happy with his pound cake and Jesus is delighted with his fried apple pies. She took the recipes with her.

Parachute

I have woven a parachute out of everything broken.
                          --William Stafford

I had dreamed a different life
as a boy I read and re-read
the Lives of the Presidents
in the World Book Encyclopedia.
Each profile had blocked out
red letter dates when the man
had married, gone to war,
been elected senator or governor.
These I duly noted and transposed
against my future that came
unraveled when barely twenty
I couldn't hope against loving men
for another minute. I lost my future,
all those red letter dates became
invisible as if written in lemon juice.

When I navigated adolescence
I found a haven in the theater.
I read plays like novels, all of
Williams and O'Neill. I starred
in high school productions and
even took a turn for a summer
in the children's theater. I was so
happy but had to work in a drug store
succeeding summers selling candy
and cigarettes, condoms and shaving cream.
My father vetoed theater in college
saying it was no way to make a living.
I pulled together enough sociology
credits to graduate. Viet Nam
loomed bloody on the television.

I didn't want to go so did what
I was told.
I fell in love a dozen times, some
of my lovers I lived with. They
all broke my heart (I broke theirs too).
Whether we grew apart or were
parted by distance, whether it was infidelity,
disease or drink, we could not hold together,
the love boat sank and we each took off
on a separate life raft. Some sailed
into oblivion and others stayed friendly.
My most constant companion
has been an asparagus fern (36 years)
that and an assortment of cats and dogs
and fishes. One day we will
welcome others.

So I am not President, somebody else is
(God bless him). And I have no awards
for movies or plays. I have no famous friends
whose lives glitter from the pages of magazines.
My fern and I have made a good life
from leafy cottages to a house on a hill,
furry friends abide with us still. We are warm
and well in Winter's chill.

My red letter dates have been pink and purple,
azure as the desert sky and jade green as
a tropical lagoon. My life has been my theater,
an unending movie, a play that makes a new act
out of everyday. My friends are my awards only
they shine from the inside out. And my heart,
broken into so many pieces, is held together by the breath
of their love kindling my spirit. My magic parachute is patched
together from bat black disappointments, stitched
with all the songs I never sang. I have not always

landed softly in friendly terrain nor have I broken a bone or been captured by the enemy. My parachute seems to have a logic all its own. It is my mentor in this adventure. It reminds me so gentle and constant: Everything that breaks me down lifts me up.

SILVER REEF

Profit and Loss

I could not know
the risk I took
my foot still slips
upon the slope
a branch broke
or a rock fell
a fail-safe
no longer there
one finger breaks
and the others let go
you know that tube
you pass through
from the airport
to the airplane
don't wish for
wisdom all at once
crown a king
or crown a dunce
bounce is neither
up or down
profit's loss
cannot be found

Silver Reef

for Martha Ham

I broke the bank!
closed casinos in a
   three mile radius
walked away with
   a king's ransom
and you ask what
   am I gonna do
   with the loot?
maybe a one way
   ticket to paradise
   a castle in Spain
   a Greek isle
   I don't know

maybe a barge
   in Bangkok
or an ashram
   on a hilltop
high in the Himalayas
   I don't care

a house by the sea
   in Brittany
   or Cornwall?
   you decide

or maybe
just maybe
I can walk away
from my luck

maybe a song
will come from
this

maybe not

I stumble
upon the desert
in bloom

if the desert
can bloom
so can I

tumble

Las Vegas
Mandalay Bay
Red Square
vodka martini
Lenin's head —
a garnish

and just before
the near collision
with buffalo
almost invisible
on the dark highway
home to Silver Reef

four condors
soar
above
the canyon grand
where
the heart of
   the world was
broken
open

Silver Reef is an area where silver was mined in the high red rock desert of Southwest Utah. Red Square is a Russian themed bistro in Las Vegas' Mandalay Bay Hotel. A larger- than- life bronze statue of Lenin stands outside that the management decapitated to placate American patrons. Lenin's head is in a refrigerated case of vodka behind the bar. Endangered California condors have recently been released into the Grand Canyon. They are our largest native birds, with wing spans up to six feet.

Neti Neti

you must go through
the smoke
to get to
the fire
-- African Proverb

neti neti
neti neti
ephemera
ephemera
neti neti
neti neti
ephemera
ephemera
sea foam
cloud bank
falling leaves
neti neti
burnt toast
false alarm
lost keys
neti neti
headache
traffic jam
interest rate
neti neti
roll call
shadow play
twist of fate
neti neti
neti neti
ephemera
ephemera
so row your boat

toot your horn
plant your seeds
squash or corn?
cocoon your light
or let it beam
all this hype
is but a dream
neti neti
neti neti
ephemera
ephemera
neti neti
neti neti
ephemera
ephemera

Neti Neti is a Jnana Yoga practice that translates simply as "not this, not this."
Whenever a thought or feeling arises that is not of the soul, the inner self
the true self we let it go. In doing so patiently, repeatedly the light of the soul
begins to shine.

Allowing the Roundness Of Being

for Naunie Batchelder

tear open
the bud
there will be
no blossom
pick
the flower
there will be
no fruit
no fruit
no seed
no seed
no root
no root
no stem
no stem
no bud
to open
one petal at a time
to flower and fade
to fruit, wax fat
and fall to make fertile
the ground
for seeds to grow
not too fast
and not too slow
life in a circle
goes round
and round
sometimes ebb
and sometimes flow
life in a circle
goes round

The Poetry Reading At Georgia Tech

leonine Thomas Lux
introduces eminent
C.K. Williams who reads
his long winding lines
and then the accented mystic
Adam Zagajewski who reads
translations of all his poems
but one

afterwards in the men's room
I overheard two undergrads debrief:
how'd you like it, one asked
the tall guy had more music in his,
the other guy said
the first replied, the other guy
had more soul and added
I wished he read more in Polish
the other agreed
they left
and finished too
I washed my hands
and walked out and past
the table where the poets
(we learned from Lux
were old friends)
sat and signed
the books
we came
to hear
them
read
aloud

The Dream of the White Monkey

I am studying music at Yale
(why music? why Yale? why me?)
off to a good start as usual
as usual a lapse, I sabotage myself
papers late, half baked, out of excuses
I must find my teacher
to ask for mercy and more time

I am waiting at the elevator
I see a white monkey looking at me
is he smiling?
I cannot know his mind
I shrink back in fear
remembering the warning signs
on the zigzag walkway
up through the jungle
to the Hindu temple
in the slit of a cave
on a hillside outside the city of
  Kuala Lumpur in Malaysia
the signs say
don't feed the monkeys
don't touch the monkeys
stay away from the monkeys (why?)
I remember a goldenhaired, grayfaced
  big nippled she-monkey
sitting on a guard rail peeling a banana
with her little monkey fingers
taking small bites
with her sharp monkey teeth
looking back at me as I took her picture
I could not know her mind

(inside the temple in great heaps
the glittering foil remains
of a festival just over
and niche after niche
of gods and goddesses
back lit in colored lights
I do not remember in particular
his image
Hanuman
the monkey god
was he there?)

I am waiting at the elevator
the white monkey sees that
  I see him
he leaps upon me
wrapping his hands
around one arm
and his feet around
my waist
I tremble
he looks me in the eye
his eyes are blue
his skin is pink
he speaks
says, "I can help"
and that is all he says
the elevator opens
and we are going up
not straight but zigzag
as the doors part
on the floor of our arrival
he gives me a little squeeze
with his knees

I find my teacher
she is young and beautiful

(she plays the guitar, why?)
before I can open my mouth
I see sadness in her eyes
and she tells me troubles
  she is having with her own teacher
that are the same as mine
when I speak I say
"I can help"
and that is all I say
when I look around
the white monkey
has disappeared

the night of the dream
  of the white monkey
I noticed as I ate spicy noodles
  in a little Thai restaurant
  five gilded heads in miniature
  of Hanuman on display

Hanuman, the monkey god
  who helped the great Rama
  find his beloved Sita
  stolen by the king of treacheries
  demon of demons, Ravana

Hanuman, the monkey god
  who helped Rama find Sita
  his sister wife anima moon belly
  the yin of his yang
  who made round again
the circle of his heart
  his broken heart

the next morning at breakfast
I am telling my dream
  to my old friend Sally

who asked in feigned innocence
  "a white monkey?"
she looked relieved at my
  affirmation
"not a red monkey?"
I shook my head no
and that was all we said
both smiling into our food

we began our careers
in human service
together thirty years ago
with people then called
  retarded
and learned from them
the language of waking dreams
sometimes spoken in metaphor
sometimes seen and unseen
  in traceries sublime

Hanuman
the monkey god
presents himself as a stranger
  to a stranger
  looking for direction
he finds lost lovers
lost children, lost dogs
lost keys
to the bewildered
  wayward wanderers in life
he says
"I can help"
and says no more
and then he

disappears

Ripple Effect

under nine inches
from crest to trough
thirty-two hours
after the ocean dropped
underneath Sumatra
the wave reaches
the Atlantic shore
of the Georgia sea island
I will spend the week on
wondering why
I cannot sleep

back home a picture on the Internet
emailed by Aunt Sally in Alabama
of a giant wave about to engulf
Phuket, Thailand finally
delivers an image
my psyche can digest
I dream of rising waters
carrying me away
as I struggle to stay afloat
waking myself
before I sink
or am saved
my body now knows
the ripple
it travelled through
was true

How to Survive a Hurricane

midnight under the waterfall
leafy branches of the sheltering trees
become sharp spears hurled
 by fierce hunters
my antelope blood freezes

in bed I am alone, no one to cling to
fear wraps my body like fishnet
shallow breaths are all I get
there is nothing, nothing I can do
weather is weather
my mind is a flashing red light
danger is danger
panic rattles at the window panes

and then that still small voice
I tell myself inside myself
to open my heart to the storm
to life, this life, to all of life
with the three middle fingers of each hand
I press soft and firm, left and right
 of my breastbone
pressing and pulling open
that sunken place in me
I tell myself inside myself
open your heart to the storm
I sigh and then the breath
 is rolling in and out of my lungs again
the breath is breathing me

far off in the deep of the night
a train whistle sounds a blue note
moments pass, further still
a pale reprise
the wind and rain carry on

like young lovers never stopping
  through to dawn
then one falls slack and the other silent
in the still of the morning
one bird sings and then another
sweet reprieve
the tempest is undone

open your heart to the storm
to life, this life to all of life
listen to the still small voice
let the breath breathe you
open your heart to the storm

VOODOO LULLABY

there are no mistakes
there is no sin
there is only life.
-- Marie Leveaux

BETWEEN THE JUJU AND THE MOJO
IS THE GRIS-GRIS
BETWEEN THE JUJU AND THE MOJO
IS THE GRIS-GRIS
BETWEEN THE JUJU AND THE MOJO
IS THE GRIS-GRIS
MARIE LEVEAUX
IS A BIG BLACK CROW
MY HOW HIGH SHE FLIES!

PAPA LE BAS IS ON THE DOWNLOW
PAPA LE BAS IS ON THE DOWNLOW
PAPA LE BAS IS ON THE DOWNLOW
JUST HOW LOW CAN THE DOWNLOW GO?

MARIE LEVEAUX IS A BIG BLACK CROW
MARIE LEVEAUX IS A BIG BLACK CROW
MARIE LEVEAUX IS A BIG BLACK CROW
MY HOW HIGH SHE FLIES!

BETWEEN THE JUJU AND THE MOJO
IS THE GRIS-GRIS
BETWEEN THE JUJU AND THE MOJO
IS THE GRIS-GRIS
BETWEEN THE JUJU AND THE MOJO
IS THE GRIS-GRIS
NO MISTAKE TO MAKE
NO SIN TO SPIN
LIFE IS ONLY LIFE
MARIE LEVEAUX IS A BIG BLACK CROW
LIFE IS ONLY LIFE

Marie Leveaux and her look-alike daughter
Marie Leveaux II were Voodoo Queens
of New Orleans for over a hundred years.
They specialized in gris-gris, magic charms
composed of a little good juju and a little
bad mojo. They return in spirit as
a big black crow.
Papa Le Bas, lord of the low,
walks the night streets
half seen and half unseen.
Some folks say he is
the devil.

Cobra Sutra

there is a diamond
in the center of the heart
no bigger than a sunflower seed
no smaller than the universe

the fire in the diamond in the center
is the fire of all creation
crucible of the cosmos
matrix of galaxies

spirit burns through matter
smoke surrounds the heart
the fears and tears of incarnation
tumbling incarnation

we are our own indictment
we turn away
we hide
like children hide from punishment

don't reject
the dark matter
it is your outline
your shadow and your shade

it will eat you if you
don't eat it first
either way
one digests the other

like a diamond
digests light
and spits it back in the eye
as sparkle

On a visit to Thailand I caught a flu and had to stay in bed for a couple of days. The second youngest son of my Thai-Chinese host family had not yet discharged his duty of providing me with an outing. Though I was feverish he persisted until I relented. I chose the snake farm thinking it would require little of my ebbing energy and so he took me in a tuk-tuk through the gas choked streets of Bangkok to the snake farm where hundreds of poisonous snakes were kept and milked of their venom for anti-snakebite serum. I had not expected to see a floor show of serpents.

The handlers' advantage was that the snakes, being nocturnal, were half asleep. Even so, most of the handlers had been bitten repeatedly and survived. It was probably no worse to endure than the boxer in the ring or the cowboy on the bucking bronco. The star of the show was the King Cobra. Through the glaze of my fever I could see clearly the flair of his hood as his handler provoked him. There is nothing more primal than the dance of the cobra. It was he/she, the King Cobra that made the psychic umbrella that sheltered the becoming Buddha in the worst assault of the Lords of Illusion: his own instant annihilation. King Cobra rose up behind the Buddha sheltering him in his aura. He/She, the most poisonous viper of poisonous vipers, is both revered and feared.

My temperature was in complete homeostasis with the ambient heat, well over a hundred degrees. The handler, a mongoose of a man, darted his head left and right. If King Cobra had detected an ounce of disrespect he could spit venom from a yard's distance and if it hit your eye nothing could be done for you, serum or no serum. That night my fever spiked. It broke when I awoke the next morning and I wondered had I dreamed the hooded cobra flared in rhythmic undulation?

The Only Prophet I Ever Met

a memory of Africa

After a week in the Ashanti capital Kumasi I returned for a second week in the national capital, Accra. I checked in for the second time at the Penta Hotel. It was a modest place, a hotel not for tourists but business travelers. The rooms were spare, clean with adequate, if noisy, air conditioning and good water pressure for the essential showers took several times a day to bathe off the dust that covered everything in the dry season. In front of the hotel was an outdoor patio where I could sit with friends and visitors and drink bitter lemon soda or Black Star beer. Instead of squirrels, black and orange lizards of a similar size scurried underfoot, always on alert for a dropped morsel of food. It was a pleasant place under shade in the morning and again in the cool of the evening. The promenade on the street in front provided plenty of diversion be it a vendor with an entire drugstore balanced in a basket on her head or young men dressed in hieroglyphed Adinkra cloth beating drums announcing the funeral of a relative.

It was January, 1991. I was just forty and on the rebound from a horrific breakup. My consolation prize was to have been a trip to India but as I was preparing, Hindu nationalists destroyed a 600-year-old mosque built on the site of a Hindu temple that Muslims had destroyed as many years before. Everyone I asked agreed, it was a very bad time to go to India and so instead I went to Ghana where I had a couple of pen pals I'd never met and hardly knew. The one I spent the most time with turned out to be a triad. Commey's name appeared on the letters but Darrien wrote them and Enos was a close co-conspirator. They met me at the airport and supervised the Accra segments of my visit. Commey was a small, compact, quiet man from a Muslim family. Darrien was from a Christian family and of the three was by far the best educated and most articulate. Enos was also Christian and was heart-break handsome. Unlike Darrien and Commey who were from the

Ga tribe, Enos was Ewe. He was also pure mischief. Their common bond was that all three were gay. None of them had jobs or money. I asked how they made ends meet and Darrien told me, poker faced, "we live by magic." By the time I left, I believed him.

My week away in Kumasi had engendered enough gossip about my return that strangers would routinely call on me at the Penta hoping for . . .well, it was always hard to really know. The economy was awful. Work that was not back-breaking and low-paying did not exist. Germany, London, America were popular fantasies among the young and restless. So when someone of means who seemed to need nothing appeared, I was taken completely off guard.

The front desk rang my room announcing only that I had a visitor. I made my way downstairs to the patio and was greeted by a light skinned, highly effeminate, bejeweled young man who introduced himself as the Prophet Michael. He was immaculately coifed and manicured. His necklace and bracelets were the first gold I'd seen in the former Gold Coast. His light skin (which I later learned was bleached) was very un-African and he later told me he felt less black than white.

Most of what we hear from strangers neither amuses nor alarms us, as most of what we hear are everyday comments and complaints. Not so with the Prophet Michael. We had hardly exchanged pleasantries when he began to talk about the supernatural. He told me when he was a child of 7 or 8 he had been awakened from sleep by an angel - not the vision of an angel but a real one, he insisted, one of flesh and blood who could be touched. This was no ordinary angel either, it was the Archangel Michael, who told the boy he had to leave his family home and go out in the world to heal and prophesy. And so he did, wandering the countryside healing and prophesying until his parents found him a decade later. They coaxed him home with the promise that they would build him a temple and so they did. Twenty miles outside Accra they built him not only a temple but a house where I visited at his invitation. He sent a member of his entourage to drive me and my friends out to his home for tea. We sat in his lavish parlor and he talked more about his work. I had never been in a living room that was decorated with cans of potted meat and evaporated milk but such was his decor. While we sipped our tea there were rows of petitioners sitting on hard benches outside some with live animals to offer as tribute. Many had waited for days for an audience. He told us there would soon be a very important ceremony, one we must be sure to attend. He said powerful, amazing things were sure to happen and we must promise him that we would be there.

Being a prophet, according to the Prophet Michael, was no easy calling. In ceremony he would be overtaken by an angel, a fierce angel, one who could not only deliver healing but one who sometimes punished and purged. I thought to myself, what hype, but still, like a cat, I was curious. The big event was on then off again and finally on for sure. The same driver picked me up at the Penta with Commey, Darrien and alas, poor Enos. It seems that Enos had been the object of the Prophet Michael's affections and had (sigh and double sigh) rebuked him after teasing him. I did not know how long the night would turn out to be.

The Holy Michael Church of Ghana was a tin-roofed, open-air, concrete-floored pavilion that could hold a few hundred people. The service began innocently enough. Junior prophet-preachers had their hour with the ever enlarging congregation. Hymns were sung in the local language, Twi, and there were some chants with hand clapping. I was getting a little bored when the next evangelist had us jump for Jesus. Being the only white person amongst hundreds of Africans what else could I do? I jumped for Jesus too.

And then it began. First the drummers entered, twenty or so strong, young men with big drums they beat in near deafening cadence. They were followed by nine tall women dressed entirely in white with white head-wraps that towered above their faces. They were moving in rhythm around and around the circle in the middle of the room. Then the Prophet

Michael arrayed in gold cloth with an even higher golden head-wrap entered in triumph. In one hand he held a huge palm frond. The nine women quickly fell in behind him and the cadence of the drumming grew faster and faster. They were whirling around the circle. The prophet's pace became frenzied and his eyes rolled back in his head. The crowd all around was also moving in rhythm, rocking and gyrating in a dance everyone knew but me.

The Prophet Michael was drinking from a flask and spewing perfumed water from his mouth into the crowd that rushed into the hiss and spray. And then as he had forewarned the vengeful angel took over and he was careening wildly among the crowd, lashing people with his palm frond, grabbing young men and shaking them silly, pushing a pregnant woman to the floor, kicking her and screaming in Twi that she was a witch.

I inched back to the periphery of the circle, hoping the angry angel would not find me, scanning the crowd for Enos, catching a glimpse of his terrified face. What if the Prophet Michael took revenge on Enos? What if he were violently attacked? What would I do? How could I stand by and let it happen? And then my attention was diverted. The nine women in white were dancing in a circle around a big man stripped to the waist and kneeling, his arms outstretched and in his hands a bunch of burning white candles. He was trembling and sweating profusely all the while the Prophet Michael was closing in on him brandishing his palm frond. Would blood be drawn? What would I be forced to witness?

And then a little voice inside my head said, leave. I wondered how and then I noticed that others were quietly going and coming. It was evidently understandable that in a ceremony that had now gone on for hours that you could ease out to take a leak. "Step by step, inch by inch" I slowly, gingerly made my way to the exit. My shoes were piled with hundreds of others but my eyes found them. My shoes on my feet I walked through one gate and then another until finally outside the compound I collapsed against a wall, fished a cigarette from the pack I carried, struck a match, took a puff and resolved even if I had to walk the twenty miles back through the bush to Accra I would not go back inside. Even so the drums beat on in the pitch dark African night.

Maybe half an hour or forty-five minutes later Commey found me and asked if I was all right. I wasn't but couldn't say anymore except I wasn't going back in and could we please go back to Accra. In a short time it was arranged. Commey, Darrien and the unharmed Enos and I were in the car with our original driver en route back to town. The driver was aglow from an evening of "miracles and wonders." He knew the story of the kneeling man in the middle of the circle and confided in us the details. The man, he said, was a rich businessman who lived in London. He had left his only daughter in the care of his mother here in Ghana. The mother was envious of her son's wealth and wanted it for herself. She had employed a fetish priest to put bad juju on him and the fetish priest had made fetishes out of the man's hair, clothes, poison herbs, and animal parts and the mother had planted these in the man's car, home, and office. The daughter who saw it all ratted out her grandmother and the father who was terrified of witchery had sought out the Prophet Michael for purification and protection. The Prophet Michael took this all in with the utmost concern telling the man he was just in the nick of time: he had only days left. Tonight's ceremony had saved his life.

Back at the Penta, four in the morning, many cigarettes later I am still extremely upset and anxious. I ask Commey, the friend I most trust, if he believes in what the Prophet Michael is doing, if he believes in bad juju and witchcraft. No, he tells me, he does not but I do not believe him. I wish I could tell you that that night, that very night, while I lay awake in the dark of my bed in the Penta, an angel had come to me, a big, handsome African angel, not a vision but one you can touch and feel. But it did not. I was not wrestling with an angel but rather my own identity, my own beliefs about what is real and what is not.

(Back home in the states I made my living practicing psychotherapy. I learned that in order to be well the toxic introjects of the past must be catharted lest they continue to cause grievous damage. I carried this righteous understanding like a palm frond to exorcise the ghosts and demons of my clients' past, and free them for a better life. I asked myself exactly how am I unlike the Prophet Michael? If he were American would he be so different from me?)

Two days later the front desk rings me in my room and I have a visitor. When I see the Prophet Michael sitting on the patio my stomach drops. What now? He is all sunshine and smiles and greets me with more enthusiasm than I am comfortable with. He tells me the ceremony went on all night long. I nod, he blinks his painted eye lids and tilts his wrist so his gold bracelets tinkle. He goes on, telling me that after all the healings had happened and day was breaking, he took everyone down to the sea and gave them a bath.

A few days later I left Ghana. Everyone I had met went with me to the airport, even the Prophet Michael came to say good-bye. I was sad and as I write this, tears still come to my eyes. Despite the difficulties, and there were many, I left a different person than I was when I arrived. Though I have wanted to, I have not yet returned. When I do return one thing is for certain: I will go one morning for a bath in the sea.

Sphinx

what happens
when a lion
becomes a pharaoh
when the curve
of his tail
and the arch
of his beard
and the cascade
of stripes
from his
linen crown
reverberate
off the sleek
ribcage of
hungry muscles
stripes opposing
stripes

the paws
always
massive
the ears
so real
even in
shadow
he hears
your questions
and being
an enigma

cannot
answer

After the Sphinx of Thutmose III
Egypt's greatest pharaoh
part of a traveling exhibit
from the Egyptian Museum in Cairo
displayed in 2006
at the Frist Center for the Visual Arts
in Nashville.

Min's Baboon

don't I even get a name?
a mention for best supporting
ancient deity?
I have held the phallus
sometimes very large
and very heavy
of the original
Egyptian fertility god
for how many
thousand years?

I hold it up
I hold it down
always in perfect
equanimity
(no hard-on
of my own
do I show -
its not in the job description)

Isis is remembered --
Min beget Horus
via Isis
Sekhmet --
the Eye of Ra
did Min in drag
ala Victor Victoria

so much for show
it was a part-time job for me
a way to make ends meet
(with only a few poorly visited temples)
it was after hours, off the books
you see

I worked my fingers to the bone
holding the scales of judgment

its like this: after death
the soul weighs in
measured against the feather of truth
when sin outweighs the feather
what can I do?
it is like flushing the toilet

so here's my truth:
my name is Baba
being unpopular
since there are a lot more
flushes than floats
holding Min's phallus
(up or down)
seemed like small potatoes
which I know we didn't grow
but you know what I mean
it seemed like no big deal -
four thousand years ago

time passes
a lot of time
and I would like
a little credit

before there was Viagra
there was Min
and there was me
Baba
baboon that I am
holding things up

say thank you
Baba

without our father's erections
our mothers would not be mothers
without our fathers and our mothers
we would still be
in that long line
at the preincarnation airport
waiting
(and waiting)
to be
checked in
to depart
in the service of
arrival
in that city of naked monkeys
who forget where they came from
how they got here
and who to thank

Flower Sutra

bulbs
shared
from
gardens
planted
again
and again

after awhile
all tulips are
red

all iris
yellow
or white
only
the wood
iris
holds on
to its blue

godbless
the day lily
it escapes
more than
any other
yard flower
an orange
trumpet
with a
golden
throat

all flowers
are the face
of life
the face
of death

peony
rose red
morning
glory

night blooming
cereus

it neither
is
nor is
not

The last six words are
taken from the Diamond Sutra.

SOS

I was standing
on my back porch
okay, I admit it I like to
(if it is after dark)
pee
outside
so I was
not just standing
and I saw
across the yard
what looked like
a pin point of light
between the slats
in my fence

it was eerie
as if some electronic
device
were recording
my movements, no
I thought perhaps
it was an animal's
eye
a raccoon or a fox
watching me so
I got out my flashlight
to scare it away
but it did not
go

so I marched out
into the darkness
still pointing
my flashlight

but when I got
near
I saw
and turned it
off
the first firefly
of the season
had been
caught in
a spider's
web
and was
signaling

free
the little bug
never ceased
in her/his
phosphorescence
and loved
my hand
and my
wrist

I coaxed it
onto a small
succulent garden and
when I averted
my eyes and looked back
it was
still
aglow

Orchids in My Backyard

not the chromatic beauties
you see in greenhouses
scions of rare plants plundered
from high arbors swathed by clouds
that tower in tropical forests

no, mine are tiny, earth-toned
  inconspicuous
their Fall leaf dries magenta
  by Spring and offers far more
  drama than these tiny trumpets
of camouflage, old ivory and sienna
almost twenty on a long brown stem

it was several years before
  I found them
and even now I must make a note
so in early August I remember
  to look
I pluck only one and place it
in a miniature celadon pitcher
the rest I leave for the fairies
lest I piss them off--
they decorate their hair
with these blossoms
for after dark fancy dress balls
and firefly-lit processions
and then, with tiny magic fingers
restore them to their stems
before the pink lips of dawn
blow the shadows away

Little Heart

I was only cat's play
low mole on the totem pole
like ultimate possum
on the third day
I played dead no more.
picked up in an empty coffee filter
on the way to my new grave
  on the leafy hillside
my heart skipped a beat
and I quivered in the hand that took me
though I did not let him see me run away.

Bad Things Come in Threes

first it was the tooth
then it was the mailbox
and then the plecostomus

the tooth had been a slow moan
for months
until of a morning
I could not resolve to keep it
and so the next day
my friend the dentist
skillfully extracted it

you know, of course
I kept the tooth
in a jar full
of rubbing alcohol

I look up from here
and I see it
I rub my tongue
on the gum
that held it
it disappears
and appears

the mailbox got badly bent
by a blow
from an unknown assailant
probably an angry
possibly drunk or high
teenager
the kind that
tattoo the curb
with their litter
drive and ride and park

to be noticed
but he was walking back
from the corner store
on foot
probably without
a cell phone
and just needed to pound
  something
and since the educational system
that failed him
wasn't available
and the world
and its treasures
are out of his grasp
his anger overwhelmed him

pound away
young man
I'd rather find
my mailbox bent
than your suicide
under the fringe tree

what do you do
with a dead plecostomus?
s/he took a couple of days
to go and I had time to think
I thought of flushing the half-foot
brittle fish corpse down the loo
a kind of burial at sea
if only the word clog
didn't enter my mind
on the third day
s/he was dead
eyeless
on the bottom
of the aquarium

this Chinese Algae Eater
had been here eating algae
more than six years
s/he had the most
exquisite crisscross pattern
on his/her belly
I could put my palm
against the glass
and the crisscross belly
on the other side
would bellow
and undulate
in that instant
I could breathe
under
water

Before I Open the Gate

two marbles
and the king of clubs

I found his majesty
this morning when I went
on trash patrol
scouring the curb
for evidence of teen spirit

numero uno
cigar wrappers
in second place
fast food
paper products
third, plastic cups
 and bottles
from sugary drinks
 fourth
glass bottles for beer
and an occasional fifth
sixth
tiny colorful
candy wrappers

and there are
tissues when
left long enough
dissolve
in the   rain

never money
not even
a
penny

but this morning
half hidden
by a leaf
the king
himself
of clubs
and under
the tossed
asunder
garbage can lid
a cat's eye
marble
with an ellipse
of orange, green
and yellow
in the center

its twin
must have
been inclined
to roll up hill
and end
at the place
where I look down
before I
open the gate

Homage to Sobonfu Somé
and the bosab, the gatekeepers
of the Dagara people of Burkina Faso.

A Lonely Six of Clubs

a lonely six of clubs
stuck in a chain link fence
edging a motel parking lot
just outside of Birmingham
taken months later
to Mother Mary
of the Red Hand
who always lives on the outskirts
just shy of the fork in the road
she lives behind the room
she works in
you can smell her lunch
and barely hear a radio
and maybe an old person coughing
through the wall
richly decorated with religious images
mostly Catholic but eclectic
an illuminated sacred heart
at the center
hard to miss
underneath
peacock feathers
in a silver vase

she seems almost tired
when she opens the door
and welcomes you in
she tells you her price
(thirty dollars for fifteen minutes)
directs you to a hard chair opposite
where she sits comfortably
in a big overstuffed armchair
a wooden tray in front of her
a glass of water on it beside

a solid brass candlestick holder
she puts a white candle in
lights it with a match
she blows out with a puff
you smell sulfur sharp and brief
she closes her eyes for one deep breath
then opens them slowly
looks directly at you
and asks
how can I help?

I hand her the card
explain how I found it
she smiles and tells me
you make my job easy
she takes another breath
holding the card with fingers of both hands
in front of her heart
she looks down
inhales
looks up
and begins

are you afraid
of ghosts?
no, my voice dips
in disagreement
she smiles and says
that is always
the first question
she asks

she pauses as if in thought
more faint music from the other side
a faraway cough
she takes a sip of water
breathes deeply and resumes

this time as she exhales
the flame of the candle
flares and flickers
do strange people
seek you out
she inquires
what do you mean
by strange I reply
good she says
then nods her head
her eyelids droop
her breathing changes
time passes
she snorts twice
and raises her head, hesitates
I hear what sounds like
birds singing outside the window
then her voice
when swallows build
you will begin as well
begin what
I mutter

she takes another sip
and another long pause
and then begins
I see a body of water
still water
she seems distracted
do I hear a toilet flush?
its time to stop now
she says adding quietly
all will be well
then blows out the candle

as she sees me to the door
holding the ten and the twenty

I just gave her
she touches my arm lightly
with her other hand
one question for you
she says
if you don't mind
I nod
why were you there?
why were you
in Birmingham?
for my grandmother's funeral
I confess
she looks at me
like I'm a child
sweet she says
she gave you
one more clue
a kiss good-bye
I sigh
deflated
by grief
but I do not cry

oh she says
abruptly
as if something
had just
occurred to her
buy yourself a music box
one with a dancer
under a globe
then she catches my eyes
with hers
and no matter what
anybody tells you
there is never
a last chance

Homage to Gypsy Ricker,
translator/tramsmitter
of the Gypsy Witch Fortune Telling Cards
first published in 1927.
The card is real.
"Mother Mary of the Red Hand"
is a visitor to my imagination.

Messiah

I saw Jesus this morning
she was crossing the street
  in front of me
as I prepared to turn left
  off Maplecliff onto Rockbridge
she had a helmet of dark hair
  going gray
steel rimmed spectacles
wore a back pack
over a green polo shirt
her denim skirt
cut to the knee
her legs purple
with varicose veins
she noticed I stopped short
to give her wide passage
she looked at me
and offered a small wave
a blessing
and then I saw Jesus again
long, lean black body in cut offs
and a dirty t-shirt
arched over a soapy car
in a sunny parking lot
next to Suzy's Hot Wings and More
polishing a windshield clean
and when I looked again
Jesus was a pretty mocha skinned girl
sitting on the guard rail
just over the bridge
hair up in a red bandana
facing east
a faraway look in her eyes
and when I finally stopped at the light

at Memorial drive
I saw Jesus looking back at me
in the rear view mirror
dark eyed handsome Semite
with long tresses like in
  Sunday school pictures

and then a sudden growl from my id
grrrrr!
challenging my imagination
are you nuts?
are you dreaming
while driving?
maybe, my timid ego counters
I am just tired of waiting
on a second coming

and then just above my head
in a higher frequency
(tinker bell tones)
a still small voice:

maybe
she
never
left

No Easy Beauty

for Peter and Carter Mills

like a cousin you
would visit in the summer
who led you and your
siblings down a secret path
to a special place
where there was sure
to be treasure
so when she loped off
in front of you
and you knew if you
were lost
you would be desolate
you quickened
your pace
you stretched
to follow
you pushed
yourself

and when she
ran on
in her ragamuffin way
and you sat on a rock
while the others
followed her in vain
you knew you were
further now
from where
you ever had
been before

you teased her
about it
over dinner
but have
yet to
wash the
dust
from your shoes

Homage to Martha Ham, wife of Peter and mother of Carter, who led three of us
(Tere Canzoneri, Susan Shipley and myself)
on a hike toward Wolverine Canyon in the high
desert of Grand Staircase-Escalante National
Monument in southern Utah.

Precious

the only thing life owes us
is our first breath
and it takes that back
in our last sigh

you have to be a psycho pomp
or a nincompoop to risk
explaining the in-between

why are some born rich
and some die poor?
why is beauty inequitably
distributed?
even high intellect
is no guarantee of happiness
fair is only
an idea
one person's valley
is another's mountain
one person's hill
is another's vale

karma like the universe
has no edge
or middle
our lucky stars
die just like us

if you knew your next breath
was your last breath
you would sip it slowly
like a marvelous elixir
if your next sigh
was your last exhalation
you would let it go

ever so slowly
like that time of rapture
on the beach
when the clouds
were a perfect hallelujah
when the orb of the sun
dipped below the waters

everything we feel
is a gift
everything we hold
is a gift
everything we set free
is a gift

it is all so precious
it is all so precious
it is all so precious

Complete

a thing is complete
when you can let it be
-- Gita Bellin

your prayer is complete
when you can let it be
absolutely unlikely
in its resolution
when you can let it be
more true to form
than anything you've ever known
when you can let it be
fine as the finest
  alabaster vessel
or strong round body of a boat
the waves lap its sides
as they sing about the weather
when you can let it be
so very, very pretty
you can't find the heart
to stop or own or touch
but be like a butterfly
when it is free
you love it
the most

Ancestor

the dead follow you
you think they don't
but they do
like the trail of a snail
that glistens sticky
behind you
when you see them
in your dreams
it is not them you see
look into their eyes
and your own eyes
look back at you
while their sparkling slime
carries you and the shell
   on your back
    ego
   out of the past
 and over the now
lubricating the future
you will one day
  lubricate
with your own
death

New Year's Eve, 2005:
Nana Checks in from Heaven

I was walking my last mile of the year
seventeen times around the elevated inside track
(counterclockwise on Saturdays).
on the basketball court below me four Sikh teenage boys
(three with head wraps, one with a Western haircut)
are playing basketball and laughing.
I had just finished an inner conversation
with an apparition of my dear departed psychic friend Kay
who often appears to me there
as a radiant head with a Cheshire cat smile
and little wings just below the ears
like the cherubim in Renaissance paintings.
(the first time she appeared it took me aback.
it doesn't anymore.)
I hear her message of encouragement in my mind
sometimes wordless, rarely very specific
mostly tidings of comfort and joy.
she fades out as in, of her own accord.
and then to my pleasant surprise
I see a gossamer image of my grandmother
more golden light than solid shape.
she is telling me that I should have tested
the custard I made this morning with a broom straw
before I took it out of the oven to cool
(this is all in my head, mind you)
and I tell her I don't have that kind of broom
and we both laugh.
I tell her I feel a little sad going into the new year without her
(she died last Spring)
and she tells me not to be sad for her
since she can always be with me whenever she wants
and goes on to say from where she is
since there are no clocks and everything is easy to reach
she can go back to any time in her life and be there again.

she can meet her husband again for the very first time
and talk with her mother and ask her advice.
she can take care of me when I am little and cute
she pauses and adds, but a hand full
and she can fish in the river, tend her flowers
sing with her friends always on key.
she says she cooks a lot
and everybody says they like it and eat all they want
and there is always plenty.
she says she can even go back
and redo some things she did wrong and felt sorry for.
hand full that I am
I ask her about going back
and getting even.
she tells me that when she goes back
to times when her feelings got hurt
she can see the hurt in the other person
that made them mean
and she forgives them
by kissing their soul just above their head
and it makes everything all right.
and then the light, her golden aura shimmers
and spreads out like oil on water and she is gone.
I am still walking in circles counterclockwise
on the elevated track
the Sikh boys below are still shooting baskets and laughing
the only difference is my eyes are a little wet now
having had a glimpse of heaven.

WHAT WE KNOW
AND WHAT WE DON'T KNOW

Blind Spot

I'd passed him unseen a hundred times
on the road to Grayson
but this crisp day late in Fall
road work barricades half the highway
and I sit parked on Georgia 84.
I'd admired the house to the left
set back from the road made simple
of stone and light blue shingles
a big oak in the yard now full of golden leaves
an orb against the azure sky.
he was on the other side of the driveway
black boots, red knee britches, a white shirt,
  black face, red hat, holding out an arm
    frozen forever

so way down here in the land of cotton
old times they are not forgotten
look away
look away . . .

we won't see
what we don't see
and can't see
what we do

how many Made in China labels
do I have to peel off
before I get it
this was made in China
Tiananmen Square China
predatory trade China
sweatshop factory China
rape of Tibet China

look away
look away . . .

O Wal-Mart!
O K-Mart!
O Target, Pier One!
so pretty
and shinny
and new!

we won't see
what we don't see
and can't see
what we do

Lost Souls of Dalian

the press of people waiting in line
the exhibition would close tomorrow
we don't know who we came to see
only what we came to see
advertised as bodies, real human bodies

twenty-one or twenty-two
rubberized cadavers
two hundred and fifty or sixty
silicone infused organs among them kidneys
and bowels, hearts and lungs
and hardest of all to preserve
brains
produced by Dalian Medical University
Plastination Labs
they will last indefinitely

Gunther van Hagens pioneered
the procedure a decade ago
his best source of specimens
are Chinese bodies prepared in Dalian
a city of five and a half million
the only ice free port in northeast China
a city of fashion and football
the Golden Pebble Beach resort
home of China's largest waxworks
Michael Jordan, Julia Roberts
and the Bills (Clinton and Gates)
on display in its collection
KFC and Wal-Mart, a large screen TV
in People's Square
three notorious prison camps
nearby

Professor van Hagens denies
his corpses come from
executed criminals or dissidents
says he returned two
found to have bullet holes
in their heads

Premier Exhibitions who leased
the cadavers
for twenty million dollars
claims the identities of the dead
are unknown, they were abandoned
in hospitals or found by police
there was no one to give consent
no one who knows who they were

with no status, no family
there were no funeral rites
no mirrors to remove from the house
no household deities to cover with red paper
no gong placed by the entrance
to the left if male
and the right if female
no cries from descendants or incense lit
no joss paper burned for wealth in the next world
no prayers to guide in the afterlife to a happy rebirth
the eldest son could not bring back earth
from a grave that never was dug
to place in the family shrine
there was no red plaque placed by the door
to guide the spirit home
seven days after death
these souls are still lost
forever seeking
what they cannot find

we find them or what has been
so skillfully preserved of them
mounted in exhibition
posed not as homeless, hapless
beggars and wastrels
but with tennis rackets
soccer balls
a baton to lead an orchestra
muscles in tango
with their own skeleton

well lit in darkened rooms
they so compel us
we hardly see each other
as other but in the crush
only as obstacle
to a closer look
morbid in our curiosity

I walk around the body of a man
see the red sinews of his legs
and back and neck
the white bones of his spine
and skull
and notice atop
one of his perfectly preserved
absolutely still white ears
the missing link
that renders it all too real
a tiny fly

Buzz

the Red Cross
won't take
my blood
but mosquitoes
will
why are they
so hard
to kill
they orbit
earth
differently
so much
I rarely
catch
them
when I do
it is an
old mosquito
about to be
sent to
assisted living
that gives
itself up
to my clap
in that rare
instant when
I win
a million more
are born
and I
begin again

buzzzzzzz

Abstinence Only

tell them
every other gay boy their age
is infected with the virus
in his spit and in his sweat
that every third condom breaks
no matter what
teach it
like the science
that god created heaven and earth
in seven solar days
and see if
they believe you
ever
again

Falling Down

AIDS is about
the rape
of Africa.
how simple
is that:
destroy
habitat
      defile culture
"things fall
apart"
we all
fall down
how simple
is that?

don't rape
your mother
how simple
is that . . .

"Things Fall Apart" is the title of a novel by the African writer
Chinua Achebe who quotes a line from the Irish poet William Butler Yeats.

Feed

you learn through a quirk
a random spike in logic
that twenty dollars feeds
and schools an African schoolchild
for a year in Burkina Faso
you respond by thinking
under ten dollars a pound for Stilton cheese
at Whole Foods
is a good buy for a gourmet
ten dollars buys the books
the most expensive part of an African child's
  education
you up the ante at Ikea
spend the twenty plus the ten
plus another five
on pretty things you don't need
forty buys a beehive in Honduras
fifty a goat in Rwanda
two people eat at Chile's
add two margaritas
tax and tip
you max fifty

the cost of a Hummer
or a rich man's tithe
builds a clinic in Bangladesh
or the Mississippi Delta
serving ten thousand people
birth to grave

you learn through a quirk
a random spike of logic
that all humankind
share the same stomach
of hunger

and the same
heart
naked
at the gate
of love

Inkadoo

the squid
is the smartest
invertebrate
both chameleon
and cannibal
the squid
is a master
trickster
whether tiny
iridescent
swimming deep
in Neptune's belly
or giant
 diablo roso
with huge red eyes
 attacking
Mexican fishing boats
whatever the size
the squid
squirts its ink
as a last resort
then disappears

before Abu Ghraib Prison
Occoquan Workhouse
"they beat
[suffragette]
Lucy Burn
chained her hands
to cell bars
above her head . . ."
"cellmate
[suffragette]
Alice Cosu
thought

(she) was dead
and suffered
a heart attack . . ."
eleven fifteen
nineteen seventeen
the night of terror:
"colorless slop
infested with worms. . ."
[suffragette]
"Alice Paul.
they tied her
to a chair
and poured
(the) liquid
into her
until
she
vomited . . ."

we are
the smartest
vertebrate
according
to ourselves --
a dolphin
or an eagle
or an elephant
might wonder
how?
Heraclitus said
"Nature
prefers
to hide."

Abu Ghraib
Alice Paul
if ever

there was
an echo

with the power
of the president
on her back
she did not back
down

the doctor
the government
paid to call her
crazy
had only
this to say
"courage
in women
is often mistaken
for insanity."

don't worship
the predator

he takes
what he can't
give back

then disappears

*Alice Paul and her fellow suffragettes picketed the White House in 1917
for the right for women to vote. They were arrested and brutalized by
the police and imprisoned in the Occoquan Workhouse in Virginia
where they were tortured for weeks until word leaked out to the press.
They are subjects of the movie, Iron Maidens.*

What We Know and What We Don't Know: Part I

we know their names
though they were only known
by their initials MA and AM
when brought to Edalat Square
we know on July 19th 2005
in Mash'had, the Iranian City of Martyrs
MA and AM as they were known
aged 17 and 18
were hung in public
in Edalat Square
hung by the neck
until dead
on orders of Court No. 19
two teenagers
Mahmoud Asgari
and Ayez Marhoni
were executed
for the crime of homosexuality

we know they were 15 and 16
when arrested
we know they were beaten
with 228 lashes
we know they admitted to gay sex
but claimed in their defense
most young boys had sex
with each other
that they did not know
it was a crime punishable
by death
we know that they said
what they said after the lashes
rent their flesh
two hundred and twenty-eight times

we do not know what kind
of teenagers they were
before their demonization
in the aftermath of their executions
we know the official spin
of the Iranian government
turned them into rapists and thieves
we know they were from
an ethnic minority
Arabs among Persians
if it had happened in America
they would have been black
have Spanish surnames or both
we know their families were poor
we don't know if they were there
to see the boys legally lynched
in Edalat Square in the City of Martyrs
or if they collected their bodies
and buried them
we don't know where they are buried
or if their graves are marked
or ever visited

we know that the method of hanging
used in Iran is the short drop
which results in strangulation
as the person's weight
cinches the noose
and after one to three minutes
of struggle in pain
death occurs
we know that the decision
of Court No. 19
was upheld by
the Supreme Court of Iran
we know the Iranian government
refused to allow any public protest

we know of another dozen minors
who were executed that year in Iran
in violation of international law
we know one of them
was Atefeh Rajabi, 16
a mentally ill girl from a poor family
who in her crazy way would taunt
the mullahs in the street, call them hypocrites
we know she was hung
for "acts incompatible with chastity"
sex outside of marriage, in other words
we know more than 4000 gay men and lesbians
have been executed in Iran
since the fundamentalist ayatollahs
seized power in 1979
we know there are four prescribed deathstyles
decreed for the crime of homosexuality:
　being hung by the neck
　being stoned by a mob
　being halved by the sword
　or dropped from the highest perch
we know on July 19th 2005
Mahmoud Asari and Ayaz Marhoni
aged 17 and 18
were hung in the public square
for the crime of homosexuality

we know the terror
continues year after year
we don't know
if it will ever
end

Dedicated to the memory of one of Iran's
first gay activists, my late friend,
Saviz Shafaie.

What We Know and What We Don't Know: Part II

we know as he slipped away
his assailant was next door
we know the color of the couch where he lay
deep red
we know the assailant was his father
who was next door in Bible study
with friends from Deeper Life Ministries
we know he died six days later
with swellings on both sides of his head
from microscopic brain tears
and subsurface bruises between his skull and scalp
from where his father would slap box the three year old
    boy
until he cried
so he wouldn't be a sissy
we know the boy
before he went into a coma
on the deep red couch
his father next door
in Bible study with Deeper Life Ministries
we know the boy
grew lethargic
had stopped eating
began wetting himself
we know his mother
who testified against his father
had not called the police
for fear the boy would be taken from her
    again
we know the father
a former city sewer worker
who came to court in a borrowed suit
with a public defender
was only twenty-one years old himself

we know he did not flinch
when the jury of six men and six women
returned after three hours of deliberation
and pronounced Ronnie Paris, Jr., guilty
of second-degree manslaughter
and aggravated child abuse
for the death of his 3 year old son
Ronnie Antonio Paris

we know the boy had been in foster care
after he had been admitted to the hospital
several times for vomiting
we know he had been home only six weeks
when he went into the coma
and died six days later
we know his mother, Nysheerah Paris, told the court
her husband was jealous of the baby
and complained of too little sex
he told her not to hug the baby
it might make him gay

we know after the verdict
the boy's grandfather
Ronald Paris, Sr., was finishing a bag of Cheetos
when he told reporters how he had raised his son
"football, fishing, wrestling matches, boxing, all that."
he blamed the mother, said "her mind was not right."
his own mother, Lesslie Hooks agreed
she said her grandson "ain't never did nothing bad."
she blamed it all on the Devil

what we know won't help the boy
what we don't know is what will stop
the beatings

we don't know how the thirty years in prison
will change Ronnie Paris, Jr.

now twenty-two years old
and incarcerated

we don't know if the Devil
had a role or simply refrained from intervening

maybe like Sheldon Bostic of the Deeper Life Ministries
who told Ronnie Jr., not to be quite so rough on the boy
maybe like his sister Shanita Powell explained it
"he was teaching him how to fight"

maybe that's all the Devil had to do
step back and let others
do next to nothing
until a three year old boy was dead
and his twenty-one year old father
was damned for life

Bully Pulpit

a thousand rejoinders echoed in my head
on my short ride home from the gym
where I overheard snippets
of a locker room exhortation
by a half naked blow hard reverend
preaching to the guys in the whirlpool --
God warns you, He warns you
not to make Him angry
because if you make Him angry
He brings you down!
referring to the recently disgraced
  Colorado evangelist
(brought down by gay scandal)
he sees me as I am leaving the wet area
on the way to the pool
he is talking now about how white people
are more hateful than black people
my eyes meet those
of another man
who looks back
embarrassed
for both of us
he is black
the minister is black
everyone else is black
but me
after my swim
I pass through again
the reverend is in full froth
vomiting verses from the apostle Paul
and I am heading to the shower
where a year ago
this same man cruised me
pointed his erect penis
in my direction

asked to go home with me
followed me to my car
then disappeared
only to reappear
the following night
waiting for me with hungry eyes
I looked away from him
not interested in hide and seek
I thought tonight
to call him a hypocrite
but felt unsafe
I thought to argue
race, religion, sexuality
but afraid of what I could say
said nothing
nothing
I cannot save
him

from himself

Fatwa Boomerang

he cannot sleep unguarded
but who will guard his dreams?

they are always there waiting
headless, handless, broken to bits
but somehow put back together again

they are winking and nodding
and blowing kisses
their whispered sighs howling
in the wind of his ear

they call his name over and over
ever so sweetly

muqtada al-sadr
muqtada al-sadr
muqtada al-sadr

we are waiting for you

muqtada al-sadr

one day

you will

be ours

The chief Shiite cleric in Iraq The Grand Ayatollah Ali Sistani issued a fatwa or religious edict (removed after protest from his web page) that all gays should be killed "in the worst, most severe way of killing." Muqtada Al-Sadr another Shiite cleric, now a power broker in Iraq has directed his militia, the Badr Brigade, to carry out an antigay pogrom. Men identified as gay are now being routinely beaten to death in the streets of Baghdad often surrounded by crowds of cheering bystanders.

Safe House

*We all live with the objective of
being happy. Our lives are different
and yet the same.*
    -- Anne Frank

*Suddenly there was a lot of noise,
then the connection ended.*
    *-- Ali Hili
        head of Iraqi LGBT
        in exile in London*

only first names
Amjad, Rafid, Hassan, Ayman and Ali
aged nineteen to twenty-nine
speaking in a secret meeting
in a safe house
in the al-Shaad district of Baghdad
to Mr. Hili in exile in London
Mr. Hili:
suddenly
there was a lot of noise
then
the connection
ended
these tender men
not a one
over thirty
abducted at gunpoint
by police also known as
death squads
November 9th
no word
of their whereabouts
has been
heard
they were probably
tortured for sport

before the Madhi militia
exterminated them
when they turn up
in bits and pieces
in one or another Baghdad morgue
will their families
dare to claim them?

who will come for
the body of Haydar Kamel
who owned the trendy men's shop
in the al-Karada district
of the capital?
he was kidnapped near his home
in Sadr City
was his head brought
like John the Baptist's
was to Salomé
to Muqtada al-Sadr
on a silver platter?

and what about his neighbors
at the Jar-al-Qamar barber shop?
popular with gays in former times
barbers are no longer tolerated
in the newly righteous Iraq
all four were arrested
and taken away by men
in police uniforms
no word of them has been heard
they are also presumed
dead no longer missing

in the would-be fundamentalist world
of Grand Ayatollah Ali Sistani
and his thug mullah minions
the fathers and mothers

brothers and sisters
of gay men and lesbians
are visited and instructed
give them up or one by one
we kill your family
horribly
his friend the Archbishop of Nigeria
the Most Reverend Peter Akinola
says queers bring Satan
into the sanctuary
his friends Jerry Falwell and Pat Robertson
say gays are the moral decay
of society
even this pope who calls himself
Benedict
can do no better
than that pope
who called himself
Pius

if there can be more gravity
in one tragedy than another
the saddest story is the one
of the two unnamed lesbian lovers
in Najaf
who kept a safe house
for gay men on the run
from the death squads
both in their mid-thirties
part of the Iraqi LGBT underground
they had rescued a child
probably a boy
from the sex trade
where he was sold for
commercial rape
all three were shot
point blank

their throats
were slit
the men they sheltered
were mercifully absent
and fled to other havens

. . . speak low
when you speak love
our summer day
withers away
too soon
too soon . . .
when he fled the Nazis
Kurt Weill found refuge
in America
in an unlikely pairing
with light verse maestro
Ogden Nash
he wrote music for
the words of
. . . speak low
love is a spark
lost in the dark
too soon
too soon . . .

first names only
to protect your families
Amjad, Rafid, Hassan, Ayman, Ali
or no names
like the four barbers of Jar-al-Qamar
or the lesbian lovers of Najaf
or the child they rescued
or full name front and center
like the Iraqi Versace
Haydar Kamel

I live in peace and plenty
my gun is unloaded
my back door wide open
my dogs bark
at other dogs barking
at squirrels, possums
maybe a raccoon
but my safe house
(they know my address)
is no safer
than yours

You Cannot Kill Me

I am not only I
but a multiplicity of souls
I have always been here
I will always be back
I was your uncle, your 5th grade teacher, your cousin
I will be your grandson, your niece, the boy next door
you can erase my words
and a new Sappho, Rumi, Whitman, Stein, Lorde, Lorca
will emerge and write what I wrote
even more beautifully
you can shatter my statues
and a new Michelangelo
with a sharper chisel and a stronger arm
will make grander statues
you can silence my singing
and a new Bessie Smith
will sound a bluer note
I have always been here
indivisible, essential
to the human spirit
firebird I am
feathered serpent
in every opposition
I am
the tender collapse
that always happens
before a song
rises up
to heaven
you see
I cannot die
you cannot
kill me

Tonglen

*A Tibetan Buddhist meditation
practice where you breathe in
the pain of another and breathe
out spaciousness and relief.*

let's give him a break
we call him
retarded
puppet
village idiot
ask yourself
if you were him
barely elected
9/11 hits
history changes
then Katrina
and her sister Rita
tear up
the Gulf Coast
decimate
New Orleans
we are
not prepared
again

he was selected
by a specific elite
to make it up
not to his father
but his mother
he had thought
with the family's
liquidity
he might be spared
the curse
of a public life

he chose
a wife
who chose
him based
on lots
drawn
who would
take who
she on the
other hand
has to live up
to both Hillary
It Takes A Village
Clinton and Barbara
Let Them Eat Cake
Bush whilst
raising twin devil
teenaged daughters

how would you
like to be president
of anything
if Dick Cheney
were your
vice president
what if it were
impossible for you
not to take your meals
with pontificating
Republican power
brokers ruining
your digestion

when you misspeak
you sound more
like Dan Quayle
your father's fool

than your foolish father
now Cynthia McKinney
introduces a bill in Congress
calling for your
impeachment
some people say
you are guilty of war crimes
from Guantanamo Bay to Abu Ghraib
you lose both the House and the Senate
your friends
forget you
Cheney's lesbian
daughter gets
pregnant

Log Cabin*
family values?

I take in
a deep breath
my shoulders
drop and
I sigh

where is my
sympathy?

I am writing
in aquamarine ink
on lavender paper
at 11:05 PM
on my 56th birthday
I can hear
the hum of my computer
and the tick of a clock
in the still of the night

when I wake up
in the morning
I will not face
the press
or run
the war
I will slowly
sip
snow monkey
tea
and nibble on
an almond
croissant

*The Log Cabin Club is an
association of gay Republicans.*

Try Another Way

face your
inner monkey
you are often
confounded
and when
you are
you repeat
yourself
monkey see
in the mirror
monkey
repeating

try another way
why not
who is
going to
scold you
your hands
will tell
you how
as they
practice
to unscrew
your
dilemma

*I began my career in human services right out of college. I was hired to open
and direct a training center/school for mentally challenged adults and children
in rural south Georgia, something I had no experience in and no business doing
with a B.A. in Sociology. Many of the people I served had spent years of their
lives in large state institutions. As a society that both feared them and did not
know what to do with them so we warehoused them. De-institutionalization
brought them back to their communities where we still did not know what
to do with them. Marc Gold, a pony tailed professor from Illinois, was a
pioneer in operationalizing concepts from the theory of Normalization.*

Normalization intended to assist mentally challenged people live as normally as possible. One of Dr. Gold's innovations was the Deviance-Competence Hypothesis which postulated that personal competence could off set perceived deviance. Another of his contributions was the Try Another Way Method. This allowed individuals to problem solve in unique ways around learning tasks. It respected individual abilities and demonstrated faith that most of us can, when encouraged, figure out how to solve problems and make things work.

Poetry comes to me often as a lucid dream. When I begin hearing the lines I don't know where they will take me. When I wrote this poem a few months ago I had not thought of the Try Another Way Method in years. In my thoughts about it since then I have become aware of my unconscious incorporation of this in my work as a psychotherapist. I believe that each of us has vast capacity for self healing. As a therapist it is my job to help someone find that capacity. I cannot teach it or even know it for what heals one soul may not heal another. My current way of conceptualizing this is that each of us has a Healing Muse, a wise and knowing part of us that if we can find it and tune into it will guide us through our quandaries and help us grow and prosper. When a client is stuck the best I can do is to offer patience on the one hand and stir things up on the other. Being patient allows the client to try another way and another way until they find what works for them. Stirring things up seems like the opposite of patience when it is really its complement, the yang to its yin. I may flood the client with suggestions and possibilities, knowing all the while it is up to them to sort out what is helpful. One of the most empowering things my clients learn to do is to ignore my advice without courting my rejection. Ultimately they try another way until they find their own way.

Marc Gold died in 1982 but his work is carried on by associates. For more information: www.marcgold.com . The training center I began in 1976 morphed into much more appropriate community programs that still operate more than thirty years later. I count as some of my early mentors the mentally challenged individuals who taught me so much about self-determination and who helped me learn to laugh out loud while I tried another way.

Rose Water

we are
all afraid
of another
Hitler
because
he still
crawls
in our
bellies

and we
pray
for
another
Saladin
who
cleanses
the holy
places
not with
blood
but
rose
water

If you don't know him, Saladin was twice famous. He was unsurpassed as a
Muslim general and he was as well a man of unheard-of mercy. When the
Crusaders took Jerusalem in 1088 they put to the sword every Muslim man,
woman, and child. The streets of Jerusalem ran red with their blood. In 1187, 88
years later, Saladin, general of the Muslim army, retook the city. He spared the
Christian inhabitants and cleansed the holy places not with their blood but with
rose water.

Zikr

god's heart
enfolds
everything we
understand
and everything
we don't

our best prayer

let god's heart
entrain
our own
in one
beat

Zikr is a Sufi word for that place in
prayer you forget you've forgotten the difference
between God and you.

LANTERN

Legacy

to move ahead
we must leave our dead
in the grave of time
grief is that slow, slow
recessional
from the day of their departure

sometimes we pull against
the rubber bands of our destiny
strain as we may against gravity
we can't return
every dream where we do
we wake up from

love lives on in love
the grandfather in the grandmother
the short lived child in the family
    that survives
the lover in the beloved
the old friend in the other friend
    left behind
love lives on in love

Sappho's Fragments

tinkle like
the one with violets in her lap
pottery shards
hung on a stick
because I prayed this word: I want
tickled by wind
dewy river banks to last all night long
they sing like
broken chords
deep sound . . . . . . lady
if only I, O golden crowned Aphrodite,
could win this lot
leaving the listener
searching
for lost notes
I long and seek after

Homage to Anne Carson, brilliant poet and translator of Sappho.
These fragments are selected and placed somewhat randomly
from Carson's amazing If Not, Winter: Fragments of Sappho.
If you need a reminder, Sappho was one of ancient Greece's most
celebrated poets even though little of her work survived except in
fragments. She lived with women who loved her on the Isle of Lesbos
and has been celebrated as an exemplar of same-sex love through
the ages. We know little about her and yet in many ways she is
one of poetry's primal muses.

Utah to Paris

homage to Gertrude Stein

I picked up
that funny pebble
on a walk
with Martha Ham
out into the Silver Reef red rock
her husband Peter
said it was just
a concretion
spat out
from an ancient
volcano

I carried that rock
inside my pocket
for a couple of years
brooding over it
like a fetish
polishing my thumb
over the smooth
ridged body
of this primeval
lump of lava
solid now
a million years

when I got to Paris
it was still inside my pocket
when my friend Stéphane
took me to
the fabled Pére Lachaise Cemetery
a block from his flat
who did we come upon
right after

Oscar's fabulous sarcophagus
but her
squat and plain
headstone

I did what
other people
who love Jews do
I took the stone
from my pocket
and left it there
in remembrance

Odd Couples

behind every great man
is a . . . great man
Ellington's muse,
his acknowledged
"better half?"
Billy Strayhorn
composed between his lines
Martin King?
Bayard Rustin
had his back
planned the theater
of the march
that made him great
humbly, proudly
walked in his shadow

Billy and Bayard
sons of the times
when black meant
you weren't
a whole man
held theirs up
from behind the scenes
sons of the times
back in the day
when being gay
made you invisible
they flashed their lights
ahead of them
on Duke Ellington
and the Reverend Doctor King
who shone bright
for all the world to see
the fullness
of their humanity

Miss Monroe

pathos in
 a white dress
sandwiched between
the pink nippled nymphet
 pinup
that launched
natty playboy Hugh Hefner
and the gouache
calcified caricature
mass produced
by Andy Warhol
pimp of fame

who else could
have married Joe DiMaggio
 and Arthur Miller
slept with a president
 and his brother

if karma is kind
and she had to come back
for another spin on the
 wheel of fortune
I hope she is
a big ole lesbian
in a flannel shirt
with close cropped hair
who women love
for the treasure
in her heart

"Homespun of Oatmeal Gray"

a memory of Lou Becker
(1928 -2003)

Black it is the colors
of the sovereignty of none
but in our land the grass is green
the rivers are sparkling clean
and the children frank and keen.
-- Paul Goodman

Lou Becker died on May 25, 2003 at the home of his daughter Sandie near Columbus, Georgia. He was seventy-five and had been very ill for the past few years. His ex-wife and my friend and roommate from graduate school, Jennie West, sent me an email from Virginia letting me know. She invited me to join her and their sons, Jacob and Aaron, for a farewell gathering at their home near Roanoke. She said they planned to have his favorite foods and plant a magnolia tree like the two big ones that overshadowed their home when they lived in Roberta, Georgia.

When I met Lou I was a big mess, around 21 or 22, and hanging on to my college enrollment at Mercer University to avoid the draft and Viet Nam. I had no therapy to speak of then to deal with my anger and coming out as a gay man on a small Southern Baptist college campus in 1970 was very hard. Lou was new to the faculty and a figure of controversy from the start. He dressed like a field hand, avoided the trappings of professordom and preferred hanging out with students. My being gay was something that never mattered to him. It neither diminished my humanity nor made me exotic. Lou seemed to be blind to the distinctions of race, class, gender, and sexual orientation caring only if a person was being authentic, even if that authenticity was messy.

After graduating from Mercer, I spent three years running a center for mentally challenged people in rural south Georgia. I had sponsored a series of Mercer interns and Lou supervised many of them. His visits were a lifeline to them and to me. This was before cable, satellite dishes, VCRs, and home computers, and the isolation of living in the country was difficult. Lou would show up often and help with whatever needed helping but mostly be good company.

My friend Mike Cass who taught English at Mercer and served with Lou on the faculty reminded me that Lou had been a fellow at the Institute for Liberal Arts at Emory University before he was hired to bring some of this academic activism to Mercer. He worked with students in the University Year of Action (some of whom were my interns) and taught courses in Shakespeare where students were required to work in the community to make real the tragedy and comedy described by the bard. Mike said Lou "was the only intellectually respectable peasant activist I knew other than his mentor Paul Goodman." Openly bisexual, Goodman was one of my first role models. He was a poet, social activist and anarchist, and one of the founders of the gestalt school of psychology. Goodman died before I could meet him but I knew Lou who knew Paul – only a single degree of separation. It was Lou's anarchist views that finally separated him from Mercer. By then he and Jennie were married and Jennie was teaching social work at Fort Valley State College. Lou started an activist organization called Eskenosen (Greek for "to pitch a tent") and they lived outside of Macon under magnolia trees near Roberta. During that time they brought two sons into the world.

Before they married Jennie was a student at the School of Social Work at the University of Georgia in Athens. We were in the same class and knew each other through Mercer and through Lou. We lived together in a tiny attic apartment on Hall Street. During that time she and Lou were on-again, off-again. I knew things were tense because Jennie would always bake peanut butter cookies and the aroma would fill our apartment. The conflict that stalled their relationship was around children. Jennie, twenty some years younger than Lou, wanted kids. Lou, already fifty plus and a father of three grown daughters, did not. Jennie prevailed and in a strange twist of fate became the breadwinner and Lou became a stay-at-home dad. This new career all but eclipsed the old one as Lou learned to relish domesticity. He responded to a call for articles from me for my first anthology on men's issues, *New Men, New Minds: Breaking Male Tradition*. The book was published by the Crossing Press in 1987 and included "An Older Father's Letter to His Young Son."

As a young boy Lou lost his father. He tells his son Jacob that he didn't know why, "for a long time I thought he did it on purpose and I guess I thought he did it just to get away from me." So begins Lou's meditation on love and loss. Lou talks to Jacob about his own inability to let love in and how he had learned to pretend to even though he couldn't. He talks about how flowers come to bloom, how a daffodil blossoms: "they open and grow because that's what daffodils are FOR: for loving the rain and the sun, for loving the bees' hairy legs and tiny feet, for loving being cared for and needed and loved just as they are." He tells five year old Jacob, "My spring began when you were born." Taking care of his son Lou slowly came out of the hard turtle shell formed by early loss and long held fears. He writes, "with you I just let myself be loved. And that made all the difference. Because you loved me, slowly I began to imagine that I could be loved. So I stopped hiding and pretending and loved you back. I let you be my teacher." Here the veteran of the Second World War, the highly esteemed scholar, a teacher of teachers, acknowledges his profound debt to a child of five who opened him after five decades to love and wonder and worthiness.

Lou was able to take care of his boys as infants and toddlers and to home-school them in their formative years. Jacob pursued his love of computers at U.C. Berkeley and, after graduation, to a promising career. Aaron, now a high school graduate with a keen interest in baseball, is beginning his higher education. He has lived with his mother Jennie who teaches social work at Ferrum College in Virginia. Aaron and Jennie live with Jennie's partner Mary and Jennie's and Mary's young son John Thomas. According to his obituary in the *Macon Telegraph* Lou's daughters live in Georgia, Florida, and California. A surviving sister lives in Wisconsin where Lou attended undergraduate classes at Marquette University.

I felt sad that Lou was so sick in his last years and regret not visiting. The image that I have of him from earlier times is in coveralls, smoking his pipe. I remember as well his candor, how articulate he could be in defense of his principles and when I sit for a minute in silence I can almost hear his chuckle over the emperor's new clothes. I think of Lou in these lines, again from Paul Goodman:

> homespun of oatmeal gray
> without a blazon is the flag
> that I hold up and do not wag.

Earl Brown, Earl Brown

Earl Brown
Earl Brown
spied a penny
on the ground
slowly bowed
to pick it up
slowly rose
with shining eyes
and offered me
his copper prize

that was his last gift
his first, a pewter medallion
embossed with the image
of a Japanese temple
under the Emperor's
chrysanthemum seal
on a blonde wood plaque
a memento from the shrine
to the Japanese war dead

why did Earl
who had served
as General MacArthur's bodyguard
his youngest bodyguard
visit the Arlington
of his enemies?
was he thinking
of the admonition
to the troops
of another general
  - Patton -
that it was not their duty
to die for their country

but to help the other side
die for theirs?

when he wasn't guarding
the American Viceroy
Earl learned to meditate
in the nearby Buddhist temples
he told me this
he did not say
he prayed
in nearby Shinto shrines
but surely
as he visited
the war shrine
he walked through
persimmon hued torii gates
past ember eyed
temple guardians
sword and spear aloft
in perpetual scowling
readiness

you see to enter
you must pass by
your own worst fears

the altar before you
is so simple
it is only a mirror
that shows you
your own face

before you approach
take off your shoes
wash your hands
lower your eyes
drop your pride

open your heart

let your last
breath
go

let your last
breath
go

Earl Brown
Earl Brown
spied a penny
on the ground
slowly bowed
to pick it up
slowly rose
with shining eyes
and offered me
his copper
prize

Earl Brown was a prominent American psychologist. He was chairman of the graduate program in clinical psychology at Georgia State University and served as President of the American Academy of Psychotherapists. He was my original therapist, clinical supervisor, mentor and finally my friend. He died in December, 2002 after a long battle with cancer. The last time I saw him was for lunch. He was bending over as I drove around to pick him up to take him home. When he got in the car he handed me a penny he had found, bright as his eyes.

Feyance for Assotto Saint

prelude
daybreak, childbirth
Les Cayes, Haiti
1957

here
to
dare

when cocks crow
politics
teradiddle – doo

you knew
voudou
juju
hoodoo

triple trouble

the road
before us:
odd
geography
a map turned
inside
out

cloud lagoon
undersea volcano
camp tableaux
a balcony
in Chelsea

vetiver
lavender
leather
and lace

arcodirisangeloa
arcodirisangeloa
arcodirisangeloa

"birds of a feather coo
spread their wings
at the edge of the world
they soar
stretching themselves
to god"

you are
no longer
waiting for wings

voudou
juju
hoodoo

arcodirisangeloa
yves
arcodirisangeloa
francois
arcodirisangeloa
lubin

ten years ago today
six. twenty-nine. ninety-four:
station yourselves

dusk
destiny
flies away with you

Assotto Saint
1957 – 1994
In memoriam
of the tenth anniversary
of his death

Assotto Saint was born Yves Lubin in Haiti and immigrated with his mother to New York as an adolescent. A poet and playwright, he was also a pioneering editor of gay African American poets. His own poems were published in Wishing for Wings and Stations and he edited two anthologies of Black gay poets, The Road Before Us and Here to Dare before his death of AIDS in 1994. His words "birds of a feather . . ." are used by permission. Arcodirisangeloa is a word created to describe how I experience his spirit: a rainbow where the angels and the loas of voodoo commingle.

Hosanna for Tré

Tré-child in this house of changes
whose gonna carry you home
across the dangers?
man-boy stepping over
broken promises
don't let the jagged edges
cut your feet
for when is life unscathed
complete?
wise young man
older than you ought to be
a stronger singer
a longer echo
too soon from
when you come
you go
too soon

in the center
of every no
there rings
a yes
at the bottom
of every loss
a voice cries
"next"
in the pitch
of every storm
there flies
a dove
in the web
of every poem
the hand of love

Tré Johnson was a poet, community activist and young protégé of Assotto Saint. A native of Atlanta, he died of AIDS in the city of his birth before his 25th birthday.

Nobody Knows Why

what a shooting star
he was
Mason
Michael
Mason
he chiseled
poems
in rocks
gone from Roan
to Short
Mountain
sacred grove
to sacred grove
his union stone:
this place is
dedicated
to our holding
together

Lucy in the sky
eyes
hair as black
as the Irish night
paper thin translucent skin
he was sweet as wild honey
and mad as a hatter
he knew before he knew
he was to be
one of our
war dead

an odd coincidence
the night
he died
that house

where he channeled
Gertrude Stein
where he danced
the clay body ballet
where he wrote
those dulcet haunting
melody poems
that house
burned down
to the ground

nobody knows why

Michael Mason was a poet and stone carver from western North Carolina who was also one of the original Radical Faeries. He was still young when he died of AIDS early in the epidemic.

Ravensday

November 9, 2004

master doodler
flower pot shaman
gay spirit chieftain
silver feathered
jet eyed native blooded
sacre coeur
nature boy
cry to heaven
beloved brother
unvanish now
raven ancestor raven
everything
that disappears
returns

Raven Wolfdancer was born on November 9th
in 1946. He was an artist, a gardener and a
founder of the Gay Spirit Visions Conference.
His murder on December 11, 1994 has never been solved.

Neil, Neil, Orange Peel

Courage is something you can't buy.
Courage is something you can't sell.
                    -- Stanley Crouch

there's a picture
of Neil and me
taken by one of our
couple friends Bill or Roger
at the Cloisters
on St. Simon's
where after brunch
we basked
on a sunny
winter's day

like every other
photograph
before or after
he looks a prince
reconciled
even amused
by the accident
of his birth
among the common folk
(we)

oh he was the kind
of prince who did
better
abdicating
the weight
of the crown
(he)
never placed
duty
before

cocktails

beauty seeks
beauty
like a moonflower vine
trophs towards
an upstairs window
(free)

the last time we talked
he told me that
Chinese pottery jar
he always put his change in
broke all of a sudden
for no reason
(spill) (heart attack)
(HIV)

he came into this world
changeling son of a soon dead father
and a bitterroot Lutheran mother
Miss Frieda, the Grendel of Pittsburgh
whose own mother
(the Grendel's mother of Pittsburgh)
spoke only German
and polished their furniture
until she dropped dead
when Neil turned five.
Miss Frieda took in boarders
to make ends meet
and ran a laundry for
a rich brother in law
she despised

after college
Neil escaped Pennsylvania
With Judi Tutti Frutti, the runaway wife

of a mean old drunk and
her enormous German shepherd
in a big finned, lime green Cadillac car
in the middle of the night
they drove all the way up
to Nova Scotia
and down all the way
to Atlanta, Georgia
where the car fell apart and left them stranded
so they stayed

I met him at a gay conference
at the Georgian Terrace Hotel
ratty and roachy, before the renovations
on April Fool's Day
1978
he looked like a movie star
Omar Sharif but with
steel blue eyes

he moved in with me
in the hobbit hovel on Iverson Street
with me and another big dog named Blues
a vegetarian insomniac lesbian witch
who slept (when she did) under a copper pyramid
and the eccentric brother Russ Cravens
who later became the ever more eccentric
raving Raven and called Neil
"the orange peel"

we lasted a few years
before love, upside down
turned into friendship.
he lived in a little second floor
apartment
with a big muff of a cat.
I lived with different lovers

in different places
never more
than a mile away

he worked here and there
Brentano's, Rich's . . .
never for long
when his rich Aunt Honey died
and left him a sum
(her husband had owned the laundry)
he traveled east and west
went back to Pittsburgh
to spite his mother's ghost
had a tryst in Paris
with a stunning Moroccan
(gazelle-eyed of Kareem)
and when the money ran out
drove his old blue Volvo
to the check cashing store
on Cheshire Bridge Road
he managed until he died
and didn't go in

his boss called me
"next of kin"
I had a key
and found him
on the floor
eyes open
breath gone
for hours

he left enough money
for an elegant urn
good champagne
for a farewell toast
and a pilgrimage for six

to the sea
that all of a sudden
got rough for no reason
(mystery)
when we put he, Neil
under the waves

Neil, Neil
orange peel
Pittsburgh boy
Pittsburgh steel

if souls are reborn
surely somewhere
a little prince with steel blue eyes
in a yellow cashmere sweater
(soft, feel)
is re-arranging
the universe
like a window dressing
for a department store
in an upscale mall

beauty seeks beauty: a moonflower
tendrils up his castle keep
to bloom and perfume his princely dreams
sleep deep, dear Neil
(orange peel)
your courage is complete

in memory of
Neil Adams 1949 - 1998

Saviz

would always sign up
for the conference talent show
he was a short, corpulent
Persian
with penetrating eyes
when he did the dance
of the seven veils
pre-recorded music
blaring from a boom box
I felt embarrassed for him
then intrigued when he
did not stop
when he did not stop
the cursor of his movement
moved me like a genie
whose lamp
had been rubbed
toward
  ecstasy

Saviz Shafaie, (1950 – 2000), was an exiled Iranian gay man who lived his last years in Winter Park, Florida. He presented one of the first public discussions of homosexuality in Iran in 1972 at the University of Shiraz (in the hometown of Hafiz). He left Iran after the fall of the Shah and studied gender and sexuality at Syracuse University. He and his mother ran a health food store in Winter Park. Saviz was a peace and justice grass roots organizer active in many causes including gay liberation and the pro-feminist men and masculinity conferences. I met him annually at the Men and Masculinity Conference for a decade. He was a poet and a dancer, the first male belly dancer I'd ever seen. My internalized homophobia was always provoked by his dances and in a way more akin to magic than logic, healed. He was devoted to his life partner Jim Ford, also an activist. He died of cancer in 2000. Our conversations about fundamentalism, here and in Iran, and about Persian culture changed my way of looking at the world. I regret due to my own distraction I was not able to say good-bye to him in person. If there is a Paradise (something Saviz did not believe in) he is there dancing to wild applause.

Back For Us

I met Tobias in a giftshop
of a little museum
where he was scheduled
for a lecture on the Asmat
of Irian Jaya.
I did not know
what he looked like
but there were only
two of us
in the giftshop
of the little museum
and he past seventy
showing his maturity.
What I remember most
is that he gave me
the look of mischief.
Thus he
enchanted me.

(people who have lived
with the people
of the forest
are said to have
this gift)

At the lecture
he cast another spell
under the guise
of anthropology.
He sang an Asmat song
fishermen sing
when they go out
with their nets.
It sounded like
the song of the evil monkeys

in the Wizard of Oz
ooo - eee - ooo

Tobias then translated:
  we shit in the river
  the shrimp eat the shit
  we eat the shrimp
ooo - eee - ooo

I got to
interview
Tobias for RFD.
He said he had
supported himself
by folding Christmas cards
for a Jewish company
in Brooklyn half
the year to earn money
to live the other
half with the
people of the forest
who had enchanted him
and sent him back for us.

in memoriam
Tobias Schneebaum
1922 – 2005

Tobias was an artist and anthropologist best known for his intimate memoirs
of life with the Harakambut people of the Amazon and the Asmat people
of Irian Jaya.

Two Little Teapots

for my mother

hidden in a cupboard
discovered by accident
looking for silver candlesticks
they belonged to my mother's
mother and father
who bought them in England
in the 60's on their only trip abroad

they come from Torquay
in South Devon
are made out of local terra cotta
from Watcombe Pottery
situated on the same estate
as Watcombe House
the same estate
where the clay is dug

they are handmade by local artisans
in the arts and crafts style
of William Morris
glazed a cream color
with indigo, tan
and dark green
decoration
a cottage on the front
a window atop the door
trees in the landscape
not a bird in the sky
on the other side
inscribed by hand
a motto

out of hundreds
available
to the souvenir buyers
among those
not chosen:

if you can't be easy
be as easy as you can

don't worry
it may never
happen

don't let your modesty
wrong you

fairest gems
lie deepest

my grandparents did not
choose any of them
but rather these two:

to win a smile from
fortune
wink at trouble

no path of flowers
leads to glory

I wonder if they
as couples often do
each selected one
and if so who

chose
which

my grandfather Wallis
was the gentlest of souls
he was a coin collector
and a quiet Presbyterian
my grandmother Christine
was renowned as
a gardener
her poppies
won prizes

so she might have
picked the flower motto
and he the wink one
for he was a lawyer too
who managed
half the real estate
in Birmingham, Alabama
he knew
how luck
could change
with the wind

perhaps each was
out to amuse
the other
and bought
the little tea pot
in a gift exchange

he teased her
about flowers
and she
him
about fate

My Cousin Beth

at the end of an epic dream
I dreamed a photograph
  of a family group
taken at Mamaw's funeral lunch
the rest of the relatives
looked like charcoal sketches
my cousin Beth
was bathed in a golden light
neither young nor old
she alone was
  looking back at me

my cousin Beth
bathed in golden light
neither young nor old
she alone was
  looking back at me
the she she was
before the alcohol
consumed her

I was six days her senior
born in the same hospital
she arrived before I departed
we slept in each other's
  bassinets
played in the same
  sand box

I thought if I was a girl
I would have been her
if she was a boy
she would have been me

together we ruled

the fairyland of Mamaw's
  mountain garden
three little ones followed her
and I had my brother shadow
we spied trolls under the bridge
  over the stream
saw the witch's leftovers
  in the rock cleft
brewed magic potions
banished and rewarded
  our sibling subjects

I remember visiting her family
in another Alabama city
and my mother remarking
after we left
that their cats were
  on the countertops
she didn't have to
  say the word
(germs)

they moved away to New Jersey
there were school pictures
and small gifts at Christmas
my aunt left my uncle
it was said she ran away
to New York City
and became
a hippie

somehow my cousin
got from New Jersey
  to California
I don't remember the story
Mamaw had a picture
taken by her husband

from above
Beth was looking up
from her seat on a lawn chair
she was skinny legg-ed
  in shorts
holding a kitten in her lap
I heard she worked
  in a winery and when
  I visited California
  I met a woman
  in a winery
who poured wine for tourists to taste
the last she poured, a Riesling
she said was "nectar of the gods"
it was, I bought a case
and wished she were my cousin
she was my age and pretty
and with a certain grace

Beth came to Mamaw's funeral
wraithlike and trembling
  like a leaf
we sat close and she rode
  with me to lunch
she shook so hard
we had to stop for beer
the drink was in her
that deep

after I left she had a seizure
and then years of boozy twilight
cancer came as a mercy
we spoke by phone
she said she felt no pain
and then poof!
like a sudden gust of wind
she blew away

(if I were a girl
would I have been she
if she were a boy
would she have been me)

my cousin Beth
neither young nor old
bathed in golden light
her hair and clothes
in pagan archetype
her smile
of wisdom, a certain grace
sought and told
she alone
was looking back
at me

in memory of Beth Carpenter (1950 – 2002)

Miss Moore

Requiem for a Teacher

I don't know what became of Miss Moore. It was her portrait, the striking young red head with the emerald eyes and the penetrating gaze who peered out from its place on the easel beside the casket. It was her mother, an ancient version of herself, seated in the middle of the room surrounded by mourners, mourners I did not recognize. A man standing beside the casket spoke to me and I volunteered that Miss Moore had been my high school Latin teacher. He said she was a member of his church and the others there were also members. I knew from the obit that she was Catholic, but that seemed odd to me. He said she had joined St. Stephen's fifteen years ago. It was at least that long since I had last seen her. Now I was looking at her casket in the viewing room of the mortuary at Woodlawn Cemetery.

Miss Moore (this was in pre-Ms. times and before she became Dr. Moore) had been my teacher for four years of Latin and two of German at Two Rivers High School in a suburb of Nashville, Tennessee. Two Rivers was outstanding only in its mediocrity. The suburb was a mix of blue- and white-collar families, the middle of the middle class, whose social lives revolved around church and high school football. The football team at Two Rivers, the Pirates, were minor players in minor leagues but were local gods in the lackluster high school. There were a few bright kids offset by a few juvenile delinquents with the vast majority of students yawningly average. Miss Moore created an island of light in this sea of gray. Her students did far more than conjugate verbs and translate Caesar: we read Greek plays and epics, studied art and culture. Miss Moore introduced us to Plato and Homer, Ovid and Aristophanes, Caligula and Cleopatra. Through her storytelling, the Olympic pantheon glowed and the Oracle of Delphi rang out. In Miss Moore's room, time and space shifted and we sat in the philosopher's academy far from the drab high school that surrounded us.

Miss Moore was also the sponsor of the Junior Classical League, a fancy name for the Latin Club. This allowed her a certain social intercourse with the students whether she chaperoned us at conferences or in extracurricular activities. She instructed us in how to wear togas and how to prepare an epicurean banquet. According to Miss Moore, there must be delicacies at such banquets even though delicacies were in short order in the suburbs of the sixties. Somehow Miss Moore could find foods none of us had tried before. I tasted my first caviar with Miss Moore and tried smoked oysters for the first time. These we ate with toothpicks, a novel idea to me and one that impressed me as sophisticated.

In the line of mourners in the funeral parlor I can overhear Mrs. Moore's conversations with those in front of me. The last in line is the secretary from St. Stephen's, who expresses gratitude to Mrs. Moore for bringing her daughter to a church she was not herself a member of. Mrs. Moore (a Methodist) gently deflects saying, "It's all the same, really." She recognizes me and sweetly recalls me as one of her daughter's favorites, "Because," she says, "you were so smart!" I smile and nod. There were others smarter but few who matched Miss Moore's passion for the ancient world. I was one of those few. I tell Mrs. Moore how sorry I am. She said her husband has been dead a decade and that children should outlive their parents. Her daughter was her only child and now she was alone. Miss Moore had been sixty-three when she died and had lived at home with her mother her whole life long.

Her given name was Miriam. When Miriam was thirteen she contracted polio; her lower body was paralyzed and she spent the next fifty years in a wheel chair. So she could sit upright, her spine had been fused. She would have been tall like her mother and sat tall in her chair which was motorized. She had long elegant fingers festooned with pretty rings. She had long polished nails she would tap on her tray when she became annoyed. If her annoyance increased she would tap with a pencil. She had a deep alto voice and spoke perfect English with no accent and with great authority. No one gave her trouble though we often tried her patience. "Be that as it may," was her favorite retort. These words spoken the subject was redirected. After I graduated Miss Moore became Dr. Moore and added Russian to her course offerings. She spoke half a dozen living languages and several dead ones. She and her parents lived not far from mine and that is how I heard of her retirement. In my early thirties I decided to get in touch with her to see how she was and to talk with her about how my life had progressed.

I visited her at home and after exchanging pleasantries with her mother she and I were left alone to chat. She explained the polio had also affected her lungs and that she could no longer risk the contact with students that might expose her to colds and flu's. She had been traveling - mostly on cruise ships with her parents - and had been all over the world. Under a pseudonym, she had written novels for the young adult market but stopped after her publishers insisted she include in her stories "elements of the occult." She had been befriended on a cruise by members of Jews for Jesus and now spent a great deal of time corresponding with Jews who were interested in knowing more about Him. This seemed really weird to me. I did not know what to make of it. I had hoped to talk with her about my writing but to do so I would implicitly come out to her as a gay man. My being gay and her Jews for Jesus seemed like a very bad mix to me. I pulled back, perhaps doing both of us a disservice.

The last time I had been at Woodlawn Cemetery was when I was home from college and attended the funeral of a high school friend's father. Mr. Oakes was survived by his wife and two sons. The survivors were members of the Church of Christ, a Nashville-based desiccated Protestant sect whose chief distinction was their ban on musical instruments in church based on some single obscure passage in the Bible. Mr. Oakes had not been a member of the Church of Christ and this was too bad according to the Church of Christ preacher who officiated at the funeral, who informed the dead man's widow and sons and the rest of us that despite the good life he had lived, Mr. Oakes was going to hell. Most of my neighbors and fellow high school students were either Church of Christ or Southern Baptist. Both denominations, like the Catholic church, believe all nonmembers are en route to the inferno.

Another friend in common was with me for the funeral. Our mutual friend asked if we wouldn't mind taking the check for the closing of his father's grave to the mortuary and we obliged. We looked like the perfect young couple and when the funeral director assumed we were we played the part. He was a pallid, obsequious man who spoke in euphemisms and silences. Had we made plans for our "future?" No? Why they were just completing their new Cross Mausoleum - would we like a tour? I don't know which of us was more wicked, my friend Martha or myself: we both claimed to be eager for the tour. We were shown the latest in the funeral arts, "the repose." The repose was a velvet covered single bed "the loved one" would lie upon. So much more natural, the funeral director intoned, it was as if the loved one had "simply gone to sleep." On we went to the mausoleum where one could take comfort in knowing that the loved one was "resting just inches away." We asked why this was better than burial in the ground. The funeral director looked down as if not wanting to say what he was about to say. He spoke in even more hushed tones when he told us that tree roots disturbed graves and then, another long pause, and then he whispered "small animals . . ." his voice trailed off. We got the message. Martha and I were not however, inclined to do any "pre-planning" that day. This obviously disappointed the funeral director who reminded us that one never knows when . . . and it is best to plan for . . . . We took his card and dashed out hoping to be out of earshot when we could no longer restrain our peals of laughter. That was over thirty years ago.

Miss Moore's funeral is conducted at the Woodlawn Chapel, a small nondescript church-like space. Father Steve from St. Stephen's, a portly bespectacled priest, presides. The service begins with a young woman out of sight singing the "Pie Jesu" from Faure's *Requiem*, a capella, simple and sweet. I should have left then. The rest of the funeral was a Catholic infomercial with Father Steve using Miss Moore as Exhibit A of a good Catholic who is going to heaven. We learn all kinds of things about Catholic practices. We learn that the candle that is burning in the red glass holder is the Sanctuary Candle and it burns all year except for the Saturday between Good Friday and Easter Sunday. We learn Miss Moore was a teacher. A cousin, a retired Marine Corps officer, speaks briefly about meeting some of Miss Moore's students in the military and that they had sung her praises. That and a schmaltzy "Amazing Grace" in the beginning and an even schmaltzier "Ave Maria" at the end, and it was over.

I had learned of Miss Moore's death when I arrived in Nashville the day before. My mother had clipped the obituary from the newspaper. I was not sad with regret as I might have been for not keeping in contact. I was not curious about the statement in the obit that she had "passed away unexpectedly." The mystery that did surface in my mind was an odd one. Miss Moore had taught us many things about the ancient world, it seemed alive for her. But once she made us study something modern, the only modern literature she ever brought to our attention. It was a poem written during the First World War, "The Lovesong of J. Alfred Prufrock." Perhaps it was the quote from Dante the poet used as preface (we had studied Dante) that was her segue. I remember being intrigued with the poem's depths, the music of its language, its dreaminess. The alienation of its protagonist also drew me in. He seemed apart from the passing spectacle and I identified with that. Rereading it now, thirty-five years later it seems a little stiff, a bit contrived but still a marvel. I identify again with the protagonist who as an aging person notices changes in his body:

"(They will say: 'How his hair
  is growing thin!")"
and digestion:
  "do I dare to eat a peach?"

Unlike J. Alfred Prufrock, I have not succumbed to self doubt, social phobia, or a sense of irrelevance. That golden circle lit from ancient fires still burns inside me.

It would have been political suicide for a teacher - even one as gifted and esteemed as Miss Moore - to have spoken out against the war of the times that raged in Viet Nam or to voice her despair over the wasteland of the suburbs and the banal culture of the day. Eliot had sensed the same thing in his own war-torn times. He identified not with "the mermaids singing each to each." Instead:

  "I should have been a pair
    of ragged claws
    scuttling across the floors
    of silent seas"

Miss Moore, as best she could from where she sat, and saw what she saw and was warning us.

Some years after Eliot published *Prufrock* he became a convert to the Anglican Church. There he found an antidote to his anguish over what he saw as the failure of love in the modern world. Miss Moore had turned to religion as well, perhaps for similar solace. Whatever her reasons, I hope she found peace in her faith.

Looking back, I wonder if my decision to leave things unchallenged and unspoken did for her what it did for me. She is preserved in my memory as a haven in a difficult time, a beacon in the yellow fog, a source of hope when I felt hopeless. The Miss Moore I knew would be bored to tears waiting for Catholic heaven . . . be that what it may. She would be wrapped in the twilight of the pagan gods, banqueting with the Muses and the Graces and between sips of ambrosia daintily piercing smoked oysters with toothpicks and savoring each salty bite.

Amazing Jean

Tell me one thing behaviorism cannot explain except God!
-- Dr. Jean Hendricks

Every now and then I see the WWJD (What Would Jesus Do?) written on a fabric bracelet in reverse embroidery. I was not lucky enough to know Jesus, so I confess I do not know exactly what he would do. An undertow in my mind makes the J into Jean (no sacrilege intended) and I was lucky enough to know Jean. Thirty years later I can still hear her voice inside my head. When I do, I begin to hope I can be as brave as she was, as wise as she was, as kind as she was. Even when I couldn't or didn't do what Jean would do, even if I got a C on an assignment or failed from being too afraid to hand it in, Jean would find a way to coax my eyes up. She would lift my gaze to hers just like she told me grace lifted her when she was just a student herself and found grace amazing her in the Tift College library. Jean was a farmer's daughter from the rural deep South who never stopped loving learning or seeking social justice. As ardent in her beliefs in behavioral psychology as she was pious in her Christian practice, she was a paradox of a prophet and a charismatic professor whose students were part of her grand experiment in prayer, tough love, and operant conditioning. What I learned in her class on social psychology was worth the whole of my diploma.

Thirty years later when I was the age she was when I met her, I visited Jean in assisted living. Her mind by then was more circular than linear. Still we reminisced on our fondness for each other even though we had often been in heated contradiction (the later she allowed she could not remember). She said we were so lucky to have been a part of each others' lives in that golden time when we were attempting deep community (an epiphany in slow motion), and then she caught my eyes with hers. I don't know if I had at twenty in the young life I could remember looked that deeply into the eyes of another human being. Jean's gift was grace. Amazed

she could amaze she did amaze many. For Jean was lucky to
know Jesus and we were lucky to know Jean.

in memoriam
Jean Hendricks
1921 -2006

Jean Hendricks was chair of the Psychology Department at Mercer University
in Macon, Georgia and later Dean of Mercer University in Atlanta. A native of
Talbott County, Georgia, she was an expert in the field of behavioral psychology,
a wizard in the area of working with groups, and a mentor to hundreds of students
she encountered over her five decades as an educator.

One Potato, Two Potato

a memory of Ireland

The name of the place was Tureen. It was named not for a large crock of soup as you might imagine but a pot for boiling the flax that had once grown in the nearby fields. The fibers of flax rendered by boiling could be woven into linen. The farmhouse, parts of it centuries old, was squat and whitewashed with a muddy yard in the back where outbuildings full of machinery and chickens sprawled. We arrived in the evening having taken the train from Dublin to Portarlington where we waited to see if Joe would turn up. Sean said he would (though since there was no telephone to call, Joe had not been told the time and day we were coming over). We didn't wait long before Joe drove up in his battered truck and we piled in for the ride to Walsh Island. The island itself was not the kind you might imagine, as it was surrounded not by water but by an ancient peat bog. There was only one road in and out and that had only been built after Independence. Before the road there had been trails that only the islanders knew. You wouldn't want to try your luck finding your way in or out. If you got lost the bog could eat you for its supper. There were many treacherous places that looked solid on the surface but swallowed quickly the unsuspecting man or beast.

It was just after twilight when we reached Tureen. Joe's wife Ursula and their two urchins Nicola and Adrian met us at the door. Inside the kitchen which was smoky and dark was Sean and Joe's mother, Brigid Mahon who was fluttering about getting the tea ready. Sitting alone in the corner was their ancient father who no one liked or spoke to. Two neighbor men were sitting at the table and everyone was talking at once in a language that was English but unintelligible to me. Brigid, a slight woman with gray hair and piercing eyes, was putting more peat in the stove making the room even smokier.

Though the incense of the peat smoke was exotic to me it was still overwhelming, and in its own way, intoxicating.

The neighbors finished their tea, strong black tea with lots of milk and sugar, and were gone. Brigid busied herself with getting some supper ready frying bacon, rashers, and tomatoes and boiling the ubiquitous potatoes in a big pot on the stove. The potatoes, dug from the field next to the old farmhouse, were medium-sized and cooked unpeeled and whole with enough salt to leave a briny coating. Brigid poured off the water and put the pot on the table for each of us to select our potatoes. Following custom, I speared one with my fork and put it on my plate. Brigid, who never missed a thing, saw what I had done and said, oh no, Frank, not that one, and then carefully looking in the pot herself speared another and put it on my plate. This is a fine one she said with the smile of one who knows her potatoes. It looked virtually identical to the one I had chosen myself. I was never in Ireland long enough to learn to tell the difference between a fine one and one not so fine and though the subtlety was lost on me the hospitality was not.

Brigid Mahon lived most of the twentieth century in Co. Offaly in the Irish midlands. She was the wife of a farmer and the mother of three sons.

It's Easier Than You Think

I saw her three or four times a year for over a decade and a half. Always in her bedroom, the bed perfectly made topped with frilly pillows, baby dolls and in the beginning little dogs, in the end old cats. She was always neat as a pin, her hair and make-up perfect as were her polished nails. She wore print dresses and costume jewelry and looked like one of the ladies who sold silk scarves or fragrances in a department store. She always evidenced excitement upon my arrival. "How have you been?" she'd say as she beckoned, "come in, come in!" and told me that I looked great and lost weight whether I had or not. We would sit opposite a small table pushed against the other wall of the small bedroom. In the half dozen or so places she lived there was always the table and hanging over it a painting of a horse's head on tattered black velvet framed in a burnt wood frame. There were various objects on the table, a changing cast of characters over the years but always her water glass, the rim smeared with lipstick and three pennies in a row. Before our behinds were touching our chairs she had already cocked her head as if she could hear something I couldn't and would often begin with "I don't know why I'm picking this up . . ." as she launched into forty-five minutes, often an hour or more of sentence fragments and *non sequiturs* that described my current states of mind and affairs with eerie acuity punctuating every paragraph or two with the odd comment, "I'm just saying . . .." I was always so enthralled I never pursued my curiosity about her process. When I eventually did ask how she did it she laughed softly and only said, "It's easier than you think."

She did explain the pennies on the table when I asked about them. One of her adult daughters had died of leukemia some years before. They had been very close and the loss had been so hard on Kay she had stopped working for over a year. She prayed for a sign her daughter was okay in the afterlife. Her daughter's favorite song had been "Pennies From Heaven" and after Kay prayed she began finding pennies in the most

156

unlikely places: in a book, under silverware, in the soap dish of her shower and she knew through these signs her beloved daughter was held in the arms of the angels.

"Go ahead," she'd say when her transmission was completed. I would take out my list of questions most of which had already been answered unasked. She would patiently respond to the mostly inane details of my current confusion. Time had altered and though someone else was often waiting there was never a hurry to end. She gave me a close, strong hug at the finish and always said, "I love you." There were times when Kay's "I love you" was the only one I could believe.

After each of our sessions I always went to a place where I could sit down and make some notes. I've saved them though they don't make a lot of sense nowadays. What we talked about in those encounters was really beside the point. Destiny, after all, is destiny. What changed me was not advice about boyfriends or business projects but being in close proximity to the light of love that Kay personified. I always left in a glow. And though she is now for some years with her beloved daughter in the arms of the angels, the glow of her "I love you" shines in me still. You see whatever the future holds, our souls are healed with love. And I know now what Kay knew: It's easier than you think.

Kay Harris (1942 – 2002) was a gifted clairvoyant who lived and worked in Stone Mountain and Atlanta.

Lantern

what is to give light
must endure burning
-- *Victor Frankl*

how is a psychotherapist
like a geisha?

we sit about the same
distance from our clients

we often drink
tea with them

we tell them
amusing stories

we listen
to their boasts
and their travails

we vie
with each other
for attention

beautiful kimonos
beautiful gardens

we sit about the same
distance from our clients
close enough
for our auras
to overlap
exchanging
electricity
leaving

as afterglow
a lantern
to light
the way
home

in memoriam
Laura Levine
1919 - 2006

Laura Levine was my mentor in graduate school and a guiding light in my early career. She died in December 2006 after living with Alzheimer's disease for almost a decade. Laura was very, very bright. Her insights often amazed me. She rejected my first paper on a personal experience of seeking help saying she knew I had a better story. I did. She protected me from the homophobia that could have ruined my young career. She advised me to be myself but not declare myself stating that "once you get the ticket" no one can stop you from being as out as you like (this was in 1976). I visited her on the fourth floor of the Georgia Retardation Center (where she worked as a senior clinician) for psychotherapy disguised as supervision. She would always walk me to the elevator and say something confounding just as the doors were closing leaving me alone with the riddle until we met again. She was a stylish, elfin woman with piercing eyes. When I imagine her now it is facing out of the elevator just as the doors are closing. I will always be grateful that she taught me to love the questions as much as the answers.

"WANDERING ONE GATHERS HONEY"

Dollop of Bliss

Ashok showed me where to leave my shoes
with the old women who wiped with one finger
a stripe of dust then touched their foreheads
humanity, he explained, is sacred to them

then we walked up special marble stairs
where slow jets of tepid water washed our feet
when we entered the sanctuary scriptures
were being chanted and drums beaten
we walked around in a certain way taking
a break on an open balcony above
the bustling street below

we walked out past the honored guru's tomb
past those kneeling hands held out
in supplication or offering heartfelt thanks
when we passed out of the sanctuary
onto the platform landing at the top of the stairs
a very very tall Sikh man
vivid in his turban with dagger to the side
dipped a metal ladle into a cauldron
and dropped a steaming dollop of what looked
like oatmeal hot into the palm of one hand
I instinctively ate it
like I instinctively took
the next breath

Be Sweet

Wandering one gathers honey.
                    -- Sanskrit Proverb

the new Tibetan temple in Dehra Dun
gateway to the Himalayas
and refuge to many Tibetan refugees
had been consecrated just recently
by that old Cheshire cat himself
His Holiness the Dali Lama
his photo sits to the left of the altar
he is wearing a pink pointy party hat
and his bodhisattva smile

you know how Buddhists love big Buddhas
the bigger the Buddha the better
and there was a really big one
bigger than a billboard
more like a missile by an interstate exit
standing sentinel on a hillock
just beside the temple

the temple had a big seated Buddha
on the inside, all golden and serene
and one up on the second story outside
that looked funny to me
not quite symmetrical
and you know how Buddhists
love symmetry
there was something over
its left eye
dark, an amber shadow
very very odd indeed

well being Sunday
wouldn't you know
the second story was open
so I got to go up
and take a closer look
that dark thing hanging
over the left eye
was a honeycombed hive
full of bees a buzzing
and honey
lots of dark amber honey

I wondered if I stood just below
with my tongue stuck out as far as it could go
and my patience keeping me still as a stone
if I waited and waited
would one drop fall
and when I taste it sweet
will a golden light
turn on
inside
my soul?

my friend Phyllis
tells a story about
her mother Pearl
they were part of a wedding party
at the Ritz Carlton
a swanky affair
they did not know
that who but that old
Cheshire cat
His Holiness
the Dali Lama
was staying there too

security was tight

when they met
the Dali Lama
at the elevator
he was the very same size
as Pearl who was at the time
a little old Jewish lady

Phyllis said he smiled
took Pearl's hand
and led her into the elevator
no words were exchanged
before they got off
one floor up

you see Pearl did
not know who
the Dali Lama was
anymore than
he knew who was she

the moral of this story?
be sweet
you never know
who you are about
to meet.

At Last, The Taj Mahal

I know it sounds selfish
but for me the story
of the grief-besotted emperor
who took all the treasure
and built this memorial
to the beautiful wife who
died giving birth to his 17th child
was the subtext to my agenda:
since I was a boy
with my nose in a book
and my eye on a map
I have always wanted
to be here

here there is
a difference
between frisking and
touching and
I am
touched pleasantly
by military security
as I enter
through a massive
sandstone gate onto
a platform
putting me
on eye level
and I can see
it all
outward tilting
minarets
and an ivory dome
made perfect
for a broken
human heart

What the Maharaja Told Me

while we were sitting on rocks
in the deep silence of his desert forest
after his uniformed militia men
had poured tea for us from a thermos
into porcelain tea cups
placed on porcelain saucers
he had said in our conversation
after lunch in the palace near the temple
under the whirling fans
beneath the electric contemporary Hindu icons
he thought Buddhism was
a simplification of the Vedas
for the spiritually unsophisticated
so now when he asked me the trick question
what is meditation?
and I said paying attention to one thing
he pounced like the leopards
who still roam his wilderness
and said no meditation
is paying attention
to no thing
so I asked him how often
did he mediate
on no thing

you have to take this into consideration
I'm sure you know the story of Vishnu
who mostly is asleep on the coils
of the cosmic serpent
his wife/feminine deific Lakshmi
goddess of wealth
rubbing his feet
so you know that in the great scheme of things
the twin forces of pushing and yielding
are always in a swirl we call the universe

but when the pushing gets too much
for the yielding or when yielding
loses her echo, fades to black
Lord Vishnu wakes up
and Lo, Incarnates!
you know from sitting on your Mother's knee
that Vishnu was first a fish
then a turtle
then a wild boar
he was then a dwarf and after that
half man, half lion
then an avatar who no one knows much about
then Vishnu became Ram of the Ramayana
and then the handsome blue Krishna
who played the flute and ravished
the beautiful and voluptuous Gopi milkmaids

each incarnation saved the day
and slew the demons of chaos and greed
before Vishnu took form the last time
as the Buddha
who said the demons to slay
lay deep
in your mind

the maharaja had already told me
when we chatted that morning
in his country palace
that he could trace his lineage
back two hundred generations
that his 186th great grandfather
was Vishnu incarnated as Krishna
so you can understand
his point of view:
  that Buddha,
  that Vishnu come lately
  that usurper

of my blue Krishna
who are you?
where is you flute?
why can I
never remember
your songs?
who do you
think
you are not?

The Bahubali of Shravanabelagola

you know what
I expected to see
after all this is the largest
naked man in the world
and I had already seen
many times as a child
the back side of Vulcan
I was born under Vulcan's gaze
in Birmingham, Alabama
which was as much a forge
as a city in 1950
towering over
up on Red Mountain
Vulcan boasts the biggest
bare buttocks in the world
cast iron from the ore
mined under his feet

so when I climb in my stocking feet
all those steps cut into the rock face
under the blazing sun
with only my 'Cricket India' hat
to protect me
you know what pushed me past
a heart attack
you know what I had expected
to see . . .
but my gaze kept going back
to his magnificent hands
and long strong arms
perfect and white
held close to his sides
by tendrils of an ancient vine
so long has he stood still
long enough for life

to wend its way up
though in a thousand years
standing
on the top of the rock
he has changed
very little

Birmingham's statue of Vulcan, Roman god of the forge, was cast over a hundred years ago from ore mined from the mountain where he stands. The city fathers of Birmingham ordered him raised to the height of 56 feet because a "pagan Buddha" in Japan was reported to be 53 feet tall. Obviously they knew nothing of Bahabuli who at 57 feet is the tallest statue of a human form in the world. Bahabuli was the second tirthankar (revered Jain teacher). He had been in mortal conflict with his brother over their father's empire when knowing the strength in his arms, he resisted striking a deadly blow. Instead he renounced the material world and stood motionless in meditation, long enough for vines to grow up his body. His statue is one of the holiest sites of the Jain religion, an exceptionally peaceful religion that came into being at the same time as Buddhism. The digambara sect of Jains are sky clad like Bahubali and carry fans to disperse insects before sitting. They literally will not hurt a fly. The Bahubali statue is over a thousand years old and carved from a single boulder of white granite. You have to take off your shoes and climb over 600 steps cut into the rock face of the hill where it stands to see it. My 'Cricket India" hat was bought cheap at the base. India's cricket team had done so poorly in the world cup matches that its members were dishonored ,stripped of their endorsemens, and several of their homes were torched.

Meeting Chamundi

I saw Chamundi
up on the hill
over Mysore
not her solid gold idol
garlanded and anointed
in the monkey ridden temple
on the top
but on the hillside
overlooking
the night sparkle
of the city
I did not see her directly
my friend Acha
who was showing me
the view
had seen her late
one night
not long
ago
he filmed her
with his cell phone
he showed me
a moving photograph
of a golden spotted
leopard
who emerged
out of the darkness
coming close enough
for them to feel
each other

if you close your eyes
and let it be dark
as dark can be
be very still and wait
you will smell her first

a perfume from another
dimension
like a lotus blossom
made of fire
do not move
or make a sound
she comes closer
you feel her breath
a zephyr on your neck
and still closer
terror and wonder
almost out of control
short of a seizure
you have only one choice left
if you open your eyes
and look into
her spotted golden face
she will shatter
your demons
you will never
recover
you will always be
safe
from yourself

Chamundi is the patron goddess of Mysore, a very old city in south India famous for its palaces, sandalwood, silks and vibrant markets. Chamundi is an emanation of the goddess Pavarti the female deific of Shiva. According to tradition two demon brothers, asuras, had accumulated great power (as is often the case) and were creating lots of trouble for the good guys, the devas. The devas petitioned the great goddess Pavarti for help. Chamundi emerged from Pavarti in a form so beautiful the demons all wanted to marry her and pursued her. Chamundi said she would only marry the one who defeated her in battle. She assumed the form of the terrible Kali and exterminated the demon brothers. A third demon rose up against her, the buffalo headed Mahishasura who brandished a dagger in one hand and a snake in the other. Chamundi reduced him to ashes. Her temple is atop a 3000 ft hill that overlooks the city she protects. The maharajas of Mysore who were fabulously wealthy were patrons of the temple. It has been in use for over 500 years and is thronged on Fridays which are holy to the goddess. A huge statue of Mahishasura, the buffalo headed demon vanquished by Chamundi, towers over the parking lot.

Why I Burn Incense

the seller of scents
in the Mysore market
assured me:
only the best
sandalwood sawdust
mixed with honey
hand rolled onto
a sliver of bamboo

when I strike
a match
to make an
ember glow
on the tip
the smoke
goes straight
to my nose

inspiration is
inevitable

a poem, a song
a solution to a puzzle
a prayer
breathed out
soaring over circumstance
how can I doubt
heaven will hear

and then I inhale
again
only deeper
the seller of scents
his sad eyes
meet mine

only the best
smoke rising
in roundabout rings
spiraling
into the invisible

sooner or later
the ember is spent
the scent lingers
like hope
after a kiss

The market in the south Indian city of Mysore is one of the country's most famous. Mysore itself is famous for sandalwood and produces the best sandalwood products in the world. The market is vast and I was looking for a spice shop owned by the family of a friend. He told me it was across from a perfume shop. It was but not the one where I met the man the seller of scents. He gave me chai and told me stories, filled my nose with one scent and another describing each as "only the best." I bought a few vials of oil and he gave me a bundle of incense, "only the best," he said explaining how it was made.

PINK ZINNIA

Archetypes

I wake up from
kaleidoscope dreams
thinking of
Aunt Myrtle's
pomegranate bush
taller than me
full of red orbs
picked more for sport
than food
the little rubies inside
so tart and pithy
you can see why
Persephone stopped
after eating just six

Aunt Myrtle
who was a little too proper
was married to Uncle Duke
a barber
Nana's younger brother
they had two older children
Betty Ann, almost a woman
whose acne scared me
and Bobby Charles
a prissy drum major
who scared
my mother

Betty Ann would chase
me and my brother Steve
around and around
the pomegranate bush
(she, sorceress Circe,
we her squealing piglets)
while Liberace Junior

Bobby Charles
stayed inside
(Pluto in disguise?)
twirling his baton
for the mirror

If you are rusty on your Greco-Roman mythology Persephone was the daughter of Ceres goddess of all growing things. When she was abducted by Pluto god of the underworld Ceres was so despairing she withdrew from the world and left it barren. Humankind in desperation petitioned Jupiter, king of the gods on Olympus, who decreed that Persephone having eaten six pomegranate seeds must stay half the year with Pluto in the underworld but could be with her mother the other half. Thus were the seasons born. Circe was a sorceress who lived on an island and had a hobby of turning shipwrecked sailors, including the crew of the great Ulysses into swine.

Feyble

I had no film
in my camera
the Indians
laughed at me
when I made
this discovery
on the white sand
beach of the island
in the tea colored
river tributary
down the Demerara
thirty miles south
of Georgetown

so the photos
of the runaway Rastas
with their renegade gardens
in their outlaw hamlet
who sold me
the loofah sponge
were never taken

and the shots
of the matadors
and bulls
on the walls
of the bullring
in Maracay
fighting
in shadow play
were only
in pantomime

when they
laughed at me
I knew they
liked me
they sold me
a spoon
made of ironwood
that will never
be empty
and never
stop stirring

Why We Pray

if your luck goes bad
get a witch to give you
a bath
get a shaman to cook
your supper
get a high priestess
to do your hair
get a siren to sing you
a lullaby
all ritual is illogical
and impractical
but when it works
the absurd
becomes
the sublime

When I travel to see my friends Alejandro and Alex
in central Venezuela it isn't long before Alex
gives me a ritual cleansing bath.
Alex is a brujo or witch who works with nature spirits.
I am bathed under the huge mamones tree in their back garden.
Alex concocts my bathing solutions from various
ingredients as common as vinegar and as rare as an herb
from some remote valley.
The process can take several hours and culminates
when Alex draws magical designs in gunpowder around me
and then ignites them:
poof pow be gone! and whatever cosmic crud
I had accumulated in my aura is dispersed.
For me the most sacred place in the home is the kitchen.
True magic can occur on the altar of the stove.
The four elements of earth, air, fire and water all commingle
and their alchemy produces the sweet and salty tastes
we all swoon over.
The High Priestess is one of the archetypal figures of the
Major Arcana of the Tarot. Her power is the power
of Great Mystery.

In her spare time she rearranges the galaxies.
The Sirens were mythical beings who lured sailors
to their doom with their ethereal haunting songs.
We use their name for the sounds made by
ambulances and police cars.
We also bestow the title on those voices
whose songs make us weak in the knees.

Why I was called Aunt Clara

I had been to Venezuela
several times before
Ramon delivered
the moniker
the boys had been talking
since Alex their mother
was a witch
and Alejandro their father
was a Darrin
I must be
Aunt Clara
who bumbled through
their meta space
intermittently
with odd gifts
and strange potions
I talked with
my eyes
and made words
into salads
I led
the ritual
giggle
in a queer
frequency

Gay people all over the world create families for themselves,
sometimes headed by an individual and sometimes by a couple.
Alex and Alejandro are one such couple who live in
central Venezuela. When I visited in the '80's and '90's they
were parents to three young men: Ramon, Jorge, and Oscar.
Alex is a brujo or witch who does readings and casts spells.
Alejandro teaches English and like the witch's husband Darrin
on the American sitcom" Bewitched" is both bemused and
annoyed with Alex's "powers." Like the character of
Aunt Clara, played on the show by the wonderful Marion Lorne,

*I was an anomaly from another dimension and the source
of much teasing by the boys whose English was almost as awful
as my Spanish. " Bewitched" had a huge cult following in
Venezuela where it was rerun in Spanish. A show about magical
thinking was a perfect fit for a culture of magical realism.
I was honored to have a role in their magical family.*

Facing Eros

Whereas sex is a rhythm of stimulus and response,
eros is a state of being.

-- *Rollo May*

the old fresco buried for centuries
under Vesuvius' ashes
shows a market scene:
a middle aged woman in a stall
selling cupids
another younger woman of means
attended by her maid
ponders them
the size of little dogs
these wingéd fellows
might be of help
in affairs of the heart
the lady considers
the one on her knee
the vendor offers another
holding it up by its scruff
a third hides in shadow
under a table

do you remember the most
beautiful face you ever beheld?
I was riding in the back of a van
we were driving on Irish country lanes
it was dusk at a crossroads
he was young, pale, no
almost translucent
he looked back at, no
through me

I had seen him before
the same only different
mestizo dark eyed
Flores his last name
Juan his first
I met him up on a mountain
in North Carolina
we were camping out with others
like us
it took us all night to steal away
to fumble the sex
for a chance to hold close
for an hour or two
I know the dark stayed longer just for us
I know we cheated dawn
if only by a breath

he was there in the biggest market
in rum scented dangerous downtown
Georgetown, Guyana
he noticed me as I looked
for someone else
he followed me
and asked if he could, ever so politely,
if he could help me
we struck up a conversation
I invited him to my hotel for a drink
he looked like an Indian prince
from a painted miniature
except for his eyes
malaria had turned the whites red
when he lived down river
and dove under waterfalls
looking for diamonds
he visited me twice more
we drank the bad local rum
he had the softest skin

I ever touched
after sex we told each other
everything
and then we
memorized
crown to sole
each other's body

my African Eros was Joe
who held my hand
wherever we went
even in the Accra airport before
my departure from Ghana
Joe was so handsome
I had to look at him sideways
he took me up to the hills
where he farmed pineapples
on his uncle's land
he cut one with a machete
and sliced out sweet yellow meat
he fed me by hand
he told me one day he would
be chief of his tribe
and when that day came
he was kidnapped from his home
left naked for days in a hideaway
then dressed in leopard skin
and seated on a golden stool
where the brigands who stole him
now knelt at his feet
he told me when I return
he will kill a goat for a feast
in my honor
all I really want Joe
is another bite
of yellow pineapple
sweet from your hand

Freddie Bolivar was wearing
a very tight shirt and poured on jeans
when I met him after midnight
on a high-rise rooftop
in the central Venezuelan city
of Maracay
my hosts/chaperones did not approve
of our flirtation
they told me later he was a fast boy
from the wrong crowd
maybe that's where he learned
to kiss so long and so hard
no translation was needed
for the words of the song
sung by the moon
and though I never saw him after
the party was over
(they wouldn't let me)
I can't imagine who I would be
had that kiss never happened

I was a Kabuki virgin before
Masanobu took me
at great personal expense
on a school teacher's salary
to the National Theater
my first night in Tokyo
jet lagged I fell asleep
in intervals waking when
the music would swell
or an actor exclaim
and tremble wide eyed
for the audience to cheer
back in my hotel room
between love and sleep
we shared all we had
and when we trembled

it was only
for each other

we followed each other from
bar to bar until we found
ourselves alone on a French Quarter balcony
 well after midnight in the city of desire
he came with me back to my guest house
we undressed, caressed
and fell down on the bed
the sex was searing
in a way that language misses
and jazz understands
from trumpet to trombone
when I woke up the next morning
he was gone
he had not hurt me
or robbed me as he could have
he took everything he brought
with him, even his name

*The fresco was titled "The Seller of Cupids" and was on display with the exhibit
"In Stabiano: Exploring the Ancient Seaside Villas of the Roman Elite" at the
Michael C. Carlos Museum at Emory University in 2006.*

The Emperor's New Poems

the old gray poets
could have been any of a number
of half or full professors
reading poems
about poems
artful and arcane

fighting heavy eyelids
I listened to one
half whine half whimper
about things that
don't exist
and the other
ever so erudite
read lists
hardly related
to gravity or its objects
I don't remember
a single thing
either said
and I wasn't sleeping
only nodding
maybe they saw me
and thought each time
my chin fell to my chest
I was signaling agreement
maybe the students who
filled the auditorium
on assignment or for extra
credit seemed really interested to them
maybe the fellow professor poet who blew
smoke up their asses
when he introduced them
was a true admirer
not a political ally

or the guy
who would or will
speak to the captive audience
at their respective
universities

I could not take the soulless interstate home
but drove the long way
through crooked neighborhoods
looking for colored lights
hoping for pedestrian sightings
maybe a siren's swirl or a hooker
all done up for the night
leaving behind the old gray poets
and the oft referenced ghosts of
other old gray poets
trying to conjure in my head
words with verve
a line with living images
a metaphor without atrophy
a song to sing me home

Heart Level

we found our seats
in the slope of the auditorium
right in the center
eye level, heart level
with the singer
she was an ageless beauty
Afro-Peruvian
raised on slave music
in the hard streets of Lima
tonight she is
dancing barefoot
to the strange syncopation
of box drum, calabash
the rattling jaw bone
of the jackass
(the slaves
were forbidden
drums
so made rhythm
out of everything)
her voice stretches
to tonalities
outside my aural range
she only speaks
and sings in Spanish
no broken English
apologies
when she isn't singing
everything she says
sounds like a poem
I wonder is she
a folk singer as advertised
or a sorceress
nothing is simple

the drummers pulsate
the bass moans
the guitar glistens
the singer spirals
her diaphanous saffron
  shawl dances
  like honey spun
and then she hits me
a wave from her heart
enters mine
and before I can recover
a wave from my heart
flows to hers
and from hers back
to mine
and from mine
back to hers
and thought she is
singing in Spanish
a language I don't understand
I do understand
the song of her heart
is the song of my heart
the soul of her people
and the soul of my people
are one

my imagination wanders
to a perfect moonlit night
the music swells
the singer opens
the floodgates of her heart
and her bare feet
no longer touch
the earth
her song is stardust

and we are her
shimmer

homage to
Susana Baca
in concert at
Agnes Scott College
5 November 2006

Takafumi

the only person
I know who ever
contemplated
poisoning me
is my friend
Takafumi
I was his guest
at a fancy restaurant
in Osaka
when he ordered for us
the most expensive dish
on the menu
an appetizer
of fried fugu fish
without telling me
in my memory
he continues
with chop sticks
dips in soy sauce
takes the first
bite of heaven
and offers me
the next

Unexpected

I was looking at the Lenten Roses
transplanted several years ago
from my friend Ilene's garden
when I noticed in my flower bed
a daffodil's yellow peeking out
from under an oak leaf, fallen, brown
when I bent to look
the bud had pushed through it
and come out on the other side
though the weight of the leaf
kept it from rising sunward
on its long green stem
I picked the flower and its leaf
by gently breaking below
the long green stem
and put them in a milky blue vase
in the middle of my dining room
table

I had gone to the post office
to mail packages and post bills
coming out I saw pulling up
a big but not quite antique American car
driven by a woman so old
I paused to see if she needed
help with her door --
she didn't
she was easily in her eighties
very thin with bird-like features
she wore an apricot colored
net scarf over her head
tied beneath her chin
her eyes literally twinkled
when they met mine
she said

"do you know what
Jimmy Carter
said about prayer?"
before I could answer
she told me
"Sometimes God says yes
and sometimes God says no
and sometimes God says
you've got to be kidding."
she threw back her head
and laughed adding
"now you have
a good afternoon."
and we went on
our separate
ways

do you ever put
an errant fortune cookie
in your pocket?
after all those egg rolls
and fried rice
it has little appeal
so you leave it in the car
as a foil for hypoglycemia
or boredom, right?
it took me almost two weeks
to pick this one up
off the floor board on the
  passenger side
tear off the plastic wrapper
and crack it open
as I munched on
the crisp slightly
orange flavored
cookie-like cracker
I read these words:

'Patience is the best remedy
for every trouble.'
when I agree
I eat it all
and swallow
with gratitude

ANGEL'S PLUNDER

WHAT WAS ISSAC
THINKING
WITH THE BLADE
OF ABRAHAM'S
KNIFE TO HIS GUT
BOUND AS HE WAS
LIKE A CALF OR
A RAM FOR SLAUGHTER?

WHAT CROSSED HIS
MIND AFTER
THE ANGEL APPEARED
AND HE WAS SPARED
AND IT WAS OVER?

COULD HE
EVER LOOK
INTO HIS
FATHER'S
EYES
AGAIN?

AND WHAT
ABOUT THE FATHER,
ABRAHAM,
GOD'S FOOL,
ANGEL'S PLUNDER?

Cigoli's Renaissance masterpiece "The Sacrifice of Abraham" was one of many so-called "Master-Art" illustrations in one of my mother's Bibles. It is one I would return to again and again as a child and the story of Abraham and Isaac would stay with me as one of my primary myths. It is one of the central stories of the Old Testament (Genesis 22) and has been the subject of painters from Raphael to Chagall. In Islam the story changes slightly and instead of Isaac, Ishmael is offered at God's command for Abraham's sacrifice.

Unlike Isaac, who is taken unaware, Ishmael willingly offers himself. Eid ul-Adha is the a celebration of this event. The story has had more modern interpretations from Kierkegaard's Fear and Trembling to Leonard Cohen's anti-war protest song, "The Story of Isaac." I rediscovered the Bible and its illustration on a family visit. I wrote the poem shortly after watching the end of the News Hour on PBS where an honor roll of 24 soldiers who have recently lost their lives in Iraq moved me to tears.

One Might As Well Be Playful

there was an alley
behind the house
on Rockaway Road
I remember crushed
coke instead of gravel
you could find a piece
now and then
with a rainbow
on its slick rippled facet
I remember rolling down
the alley
in refrigerator boxes
with friends tumbling
laughing
squealing like
little pigs
and the look of horror
on my mother's face
when she found me
with my hands
in a nest
of baby serpents
whose mother
was
a rattlesnake
"big worms!"
I exclaimed
as she swooped
down with enough
calm
and enough
alacrity
that I let go
unbitten

and was taken
by her
trembling
to safety
where
she held me
and wept softly
for reasons
I could not
understand

Murray Gell-Mann was a physicist who coined the term "quark" based on James Joyce's play on the call of seabirds in Finnegan's Wake:
    "Three quarks for Muster Mark
    Sure he has not got much of a bark
    And sure he has it's all beside the mark."

When asked about the six different types of quark up, down, charm, strange, top and bottom, also terms he coined he said,
    "The terms are just for fun.
    There's no particular reason to use pompous names.
    One might as well be playful".

Coke according to Wikepedia is "a carbonaceous material derived from the destructive distillation of low ash, low sulfur bituminous coal." Where I grew up, Birmingham, Alabama there were lots of steel mills and the by-product, coke was plentiful and used as paving material.

The part about the snakes and my mother: I cannot swear to the veracity of my memory. I often quote my dear friend Edith Kelman who once said, "My memory has an imagination."

Gravity and the Boy

the writhing
was the worst of it
I was to do what
my grandmother did
when she stomped
it dead
only my little foot
just half killed it
I'd have to look
to see the broken
black and orange
body of a large
grasshopper
who would have eaten
my grandmother's
daylilies
and my grandfather's
tomatoes
so it had to be
stomped on
though
I hated it
and hated it
worse
when it
did not die

Gravity and the Man

I knew
I'd meet
that snake again
and that's why
I did not
want
to
kill it
but you can't let
a large poisonous snake
live under your porch --
how I did it
is a story
for another day
that snake I met
in the Ozarks
had the same
glint of eye
it warned me
not with its rattle
but its penetrating
gaze
it offered me nothing
and what it asked for
I can't talk about
but when I was finished
and turned and walked
  away
it let me go

Ouroboros

so allow
the holy
moment
to be
how
in the
tingle
of our
light
bodies
we are
always
meeting
each
other
just where
we left
off
and so
begin
. . .

*Ouroboros
is a snake
eating its own
tail.
a symbol of
the cosmic circle
/cycle.
like this poem
a Mobius strip
always folding back
into itself*
. . .

Inevitable

a red-tailed hawk
landed on my garden gate.
standing in front
of my back door
I stared back at the bird.
undone in chthonic chartreuse eyes
for as long as it takes
to register
he or she
looked back at me
and so I said
Great One
please
do not eat
or otherwise
menace
my little
dogs.
she or he
did not fly away
but looked back at me
with no apology.

I telepath
are we agreed?
I will sling
no stone
and you will circle
like an angel
of mercy
waiting
as mercy waits . . .
wing spans over
abundant shoulders
for rivers

of tears
when grief
meets joy

Tickled to Death

finally the angelfairies
that had followed
Eloise since she
was planted in her Mama's
WOMB
begin tickling with tiny fingers so
Eloise felt like she had been kissed
by a thousand butterflies
they joined their wings into a golden net
and slowly ever so slowly hoisted her up
from the wreck of her body
then they circled in a trampoline
of light
and bounced her blithe spirit
off to another star

for all our Eloises

My Eloise is a visitor to my imagination.
"Tickled to death" as an old timey
expression of joy.

Watching a Peony Bloom

three dollars a stem
is an extravagance
for me
the lie I told
myself
to justify -
it will open
fully in a week
for my birthday
the truth -
the ones I grow
and pick
in the opposite
season
were a gift
from someone
who now
an angel
will enjoy
with me
the pop
the spread
the pink perfume

Full Moon Haiku

double swoon
the moon's
a gold doubloon
in a charcoal sky
double sigh

The Beach is Never the Same Beach

the beach is never the same beach
the morning beach is not the evening beach
   ten years later everything is different
only the compass of intuition can take me
   to the spot, the point of departure
the place where we entered the waters
   that had been so placid until we let you go
in the sudden mad toss of the tides that pulled us
   to and fro and around and around in a merry scary circle
this afternoon the beach glitters white light under the winter sun
   the aquamarine waters are translucent and calm
I walk away from the friends I came with who knew you too
   pulled in one direction filling my lungs with the salt air
salt running down my cheeks, I miss you old friend I say in tears
   and then I turn and return looking down for an omen
a special shell, a piece of polished glass,
   the arrowhead tooth of a shark
   what comes to me comes from above,
   the shadow of a gull flying low
just over my head and I hear the wings of your voice
   between the waves,
   "all is well." you land twenty feet back from where I stand
letting me know you know
   I was there in the place where I let you go

*My friend Neil Adams died March 4, 1998 and that summer friends Bill, Roger,
Martin, Frank, Everett and I went to the Grayton Beach on the Gulf of Mexico
on the Florida panhandle to scatter Neil's ashes in the sea. I had not returned
since then. Ten years later I did go back for a psychology conference in nearby
Sandestin. After the conference friends Ilene, Russ and I stopped at Santa
Rosa Beach and I tried to find the spot where a decade before Neil's remains
were given to the waves. Neil loved that stretch of beach and spent some of his
happiest times there.*

Milky Way

like a lump of sugar
in a cup of milk
when my time is nigh
may I dissolve
into the mother light
that gave me birth
(where I belong
in the Milky Way)
when I see the light
may I not blink
in the face of love
but let myself go
all of me
every particle
into that
abiding wave

Valley of the Gods

sun rises
over ancient cenotaphs
of desert gods
eating all
the pink of dawn
young rabbits
run willy nilly
in the sage brush
bright eyed
I rise too
and my heart
follows them

for Martha Ham
who took me there

A Prayer for Jude

before there was email
there was prayer
before I could forward
  anything
I would hold in my heart
  all of my love
  and concern
  and when I could
instead of instant messaging
  I let it all
  go to god

*Jude St. Martin was born in 1961 in New Orleans, lived many years in Atlanta
before moving to New York City seven years ago where he died in July 2008.
Jude was a self-educated poet and philosopher, body builder, masseur and
personal trainer. He loved his divas and wrote a fifty page poem to Aretha
Franklin. He would often play Edith Piaf during a massage session. Passionate
about all things spiritual he was in constant dialogue with a god he wasn't sure
existed. If Jude is with God now I bet they are having a heated conversation. I
hope Jude is finally getting some of his burning questions answered and that
God is getting an amazing massage listening between the questions to the Little
Sparrow sing La Vie en Rose.*

Duermevela

A disbelief in magic can force a pour soul
into believing in government and business.
                    -- Tom Robbins

there is some golden place
I am still looking for
I have seen it in dream
  after dream
  I have seen it
shimmer
on the surface of the water
shimmer
in my aura in the mirror
I can hear it
between ticks
of the clock
tic-toc
in the mist between
me and the dark
it barks
and falls silent
again and again
it is in between
all my molecules
I am it opening
as a flower
to the sun

for my writing group, the Ninth Muse

www.theninthmuse.com

Duermevela is a Spanish word with no English equivalent.
It refers to those spaces between sleeping and waking
where the world of dreams commingles with the world of forms.

Aretha's Hat

my favorite inaugural image:
Aretha's hat
gray wool felt studded
with Swavorski crystals
purchased in Detroit
for one hundred and
seventy-nine dollars
from Mr. Song Millinery
warmed her head
that chilly day

crown jewels for
the Queen of Soul?
no need with a voice
that shines like diamonds
that shimmers opalescent
her song
a string of pearls

Pink Zinnia

only one
oddly placed
in an unlikely crack
between
a driveway
and the sidewalk
seen at a glance
driving to work
in early October
Summer's supposed
to be over
but there
persistent
pink petaled
just the kind
of flower
my Nana
grew the
most of
though she
loved them
less than roses
their drought
resistant
tough stemmed
architecture
gave her
continuous
color she
never
tired
of arranging
shapes
and sizes
of the zinnia

family
she loved
pink the best
and there she was
oddly placed
lasting longer than
her season
winking
back
at me

LaVergne, TN USA
27 August 2010
194878LV00003B/42/P